MW00760661

PRAISE FOR
LIVE AN EXTRAORDINARY LIFE

"Many people have a dream of what their extraordinary life will look like, and they believe what makes it extraordinary is the end result. But in this book, David Bush does a great job of debunking the idea that being extraordinary is based solely on our level of accomplishments. He inspires us to realize having an extraordinary life is based on being driven by passion and purpose. It's how we live every day, how we think about the task in front of us, and our commitment to being extraordinary! Do you want to live an Extraordinary Life? I have never heard anyone say, NO, to this question, so why do so few actually do it? In my experience, it is because they do not know the everyday steps to take to make their life extraordinary. Well, look no further. In *Live an Extraordinary Life*, David Bush lays out a comprehensive, easy-to-follow guide on how to build and carry out YOUR extraordinary life. If you responded "yes" to the above question (which I am assuming was all of you), this book is a must-read! Stop waiting on your dream to just happen; pick up a copy of this book today and make the extraordinary happen!"

> **KURT WARNER**, author of *All Things Possible*, Pro Football Hall of Fame Quarterback, Super Bowl XXX-IV Champion, Super Bowl (XXXIV MVP, 2x NFL Most Valuable Player (1999, 2001), and Walter Payton NFL Man of the Year (2008)

"David Bush's book provides a step-by-step plan to achieve extraordinary results in everything you do, and it will empower you to break through old habits to live an Extraordinary Life!"

> **JON GORDON**, author of twenty-four books including *The Energy Bus, Training Camp,* and twelve best sellers

"David definitely hit the mark with this book! From time to time, everyone needs inspiration to take life to the next level. This book does that and a whole lot more. Within the first five minutes of reading, I was already being personally challenged to answer some thought-provoking questions about whether or not I'm stuck being a 'comfort cave camper' or if I'm still pursuing my next life goals. David's step-by-step guide is a great tool for achieving your own Extraordinary Life."

> **JON DEVORE**, professional skydiving stuntman, aerial stunt coordinator, and aerial cinematographer with more than 22,000 skydives and BASE/Wing Suit BASE jumps, two-time World Champion, aerial stunt coordinator, and manager of the Red Bull Air Force for the past nineteen years

"This wonderful, warm, inspiring book shows you a series of practical, proven methods and techniques that you can use immediately to set and achieve all your goals. You learn how to become everything you were meant to become."

> **BRIAN TRACY**, author of ninety-one books and chairman and CEO of Brian Tracy International, a company specializing in the training and development of individuals and organizations

"When I opened up this book I started reading and simply couldn't put it down! David Bush is an excellent writer, storyteller and life coach. He has successfully accomplished these goals in his own life and is sharing the principles with the reader having developed a proven model for personal success. *Live an Extraordinary Life* Book will show you where you are at and how to change your life, one decision at a time, attain your dreams, and experience a successful life no matter what you haven't achieved — yet! I asked myself, Who is this book not for?, And I couldn't come up with anyone! This book will help you, your peers, your adult children, adult grandchildren, and anyone who needs a trusted life coach to show them how they have the power to make decisions and accomplish their personal goals and dreams in a myriad of areas. I consider David Bush a personal friend and truly a wonderful life coach."

DRS. GARY AND BARBARA ROSBERG, cofounders of America's Family Coaches, authors of over thirteen books, including the Gold Medallion Award-winning Marriage Book of the Year in Christian publishing, *The 6 Secrets to a Lasting Love*. Together they are Executive Marriage Coaches, and Barbara is the CEO of The Rosberg Group. The couple are authors and presenters of numerous videos on marriage, the faculty, and the board of reference for the International Christian Coaching Institute, providing certifications in coaching worldwide

"David Bush is EXTRAordinary! Once, he was significantly overweight even though he had been a professional football player. In addition, he had problems with his finances, relationships, and attitude. However, David realized he was living a less-than-extraordinary life and decided to turn his life around to achieve his current successful extraordinary life as a Peak Performance Coach. In his new book, *Live an Extraordinary Life*, David shares his step-by-step strategies to create a lasting impact and a legacy that casts your shadow beyond the grave."

DR. TONY ALESSANDRA, author of The Platinum Rule® and *The NEW Art of Managing People*

"The best way to find and live your calling is to follow in the footsteps of someone already living authentically and fully. Dave's book contains a succinct and workable blueprint to help you achieve what you truly desire. Read it and begin living your extraordinary life!"

DR. TRACEY C. JONES, MBA, PhD, author of *SPARK: Five Essentials to Igniting the Greatness Within*

"The six commitments that will lead to your extraordinary life are not taught in school or observed in the common man. But fortunately, they are not 'secrets' that are hidden from us. Here is your blueprint for separating yourself from the common and the ordinary. Like Sir Edmund Hillary, you can choose to conquer yourself and live an extraordinary life."

DAN MILLER, author of the *New York Times* best-selling *48 Days To The Work (And Life) You Love, No More Dreaded Mondays,* and *Wisdom Meets Passion*

"This book is a rich gold mine for people who aspire to lead an extraordinary life. I have seen Dave in action, and I am in awe of how many lives he has positively impacted. After a conversation with one of our participants at our Mindset workshop, she took his advice and set a more ambitious life goal. Two years later, she earns over $100,000 more a year than in her old job. Another participant lost an astonishing ninety punds in six months. His life was transformed. David's new book can help you unlock the magic that's already within you. Don't miss reading this book. Without Dave's great book, you may miss your true destiny."

GERHARD GSCHWANDTNER, CEO of SellingPower.com

"David Bush is extraordinary! When I first met David there was something different about him. He lives his life as a model for others, then writes a book to help simplify the steps. He is one of those people you want to spend more time with! We were only given one life to live — let's all do it EXTRAordinarily!"

ADAM TIMMERMAN, two-tine NFL Super Bowl Champion and All Pro Offensive Lineman for Green Bay Packers and St. Louis Rams

"It's one thing to make a living, but quite another to make a life — particularly one that is extraordinary. My good friend David Bush.

I spent a lifetime studying and living out the principles he lays out in this extremely practical book. As an accomplished high-performance coach who knows how to help people make a great life and living, David delivers practical insights that I've seen him put to work in his life and in the lives of hundreds of others over the years. If you want an extraordinary life that is productive, profitable, fulfilling, joyful, and impactful, read his book and put it to work."

DR. RON JENSON, author of twenty-four books, international convention speaker, and known around the world as "America's Life Coach"

"There are those who wake up each morning without a plan or purpose, then there is David Bush! He is the perfect example of someone who realizes what they no longer will accept, identifies what they want, and then GOES FOR IT without a thought of giving up! When I first met David face-to-face, he drove for hours to meet with me on my yacht. I knew right then that this was someone who was going somewhere and, most importantly, someone that I could trust 100 percent! David has put his heart and soul into this book, along with the secrets that have made him who he is today. And it's not just a book to read, but a workbook of sorts that will keep you involved so that you evolve each time you turn a page. When finished, you will have a new outlook on life with a plan for the 'future you' that you have been wanting to meet, living the Extraordinary Life you were born to live!"

HENRY A. PENIX, international author, speaker, and entrepreneur, and CEO and cofounder of Soaak Technologies, Inc., a digitized mental health and wellness solution accessible from any mobile device

"David Bush and I met in 2008. I felt immediate warmth and sincerity from this smart and engaging man. Since then, I've had a front row seat listening to David teach and share his *Live An Ex-*

traordinary Life message and method. More importantly, I still see him strategically live out the good, bad, and ugly with unabashed boldness for all to see.

Why is David able to be so vulnerable, passionate, and accomplished at expressing his calling? As avid and accomplished as he is at pouring wisdom and experience into others, he's extraordinarily curious and coachable (Chapter 5, Expand Your Perspective).

Being a quick learner and thoughtful leader, David's willingness to risk 'failing' fast and adapt translates to finding a way that produces results. This remarkable trait is exceeded only by his generous dropping of breadcrumbs for the rest of us to follow. In *Live An Extraordinary Life,* David hands us the loaf of bread and says, 'Join me. Now, it's your turn to make the Six Extraordinary Commitments.'"

> **KEVIN W. MCCARTHY**, author of *The On-Purpose Person* and creator of ONPURPOSE.me for finding your purpose in life

"The world is full of 'success' stories written by people who were born on third and thought they hit a triple. Dave's story is different. I met Dave when he was fresh out of college and was immediately impressed by his desire to live an extraordinary life. Even then, he had set his goals to not just find his significance, but he was determined to help others do the same. Dave began with nothing but a dream as he sought to discover, refine, practice, fail, and try again to develop, through repetition and practice, the principles of Extraordinary Living. Thousands have used these principles to forge a different course out of complacency and into extraordinary outcomes, and you can too! If you have ever desired to be mentored by someone dedicated to your success in every area of your life, this is your chance to be coached by one of the best!"

> **PAT SOKOLL**, life and relationship coach, The Connection Company

"I have had the great privilege of working with, and personally knowing, David Bush for well over a decade. I have coached and mentored hundreds of executives and millions of professionals in my career, and I can tell you that David Bush stands out as one of the best leaders I have ever had the honor to work with. David is simply the real deal. He does not just write and speak about healthy living and life balance, but he exemplifies it in his own life and possesses a level of integrity and care for others that is rare! This book is a must-read for anyone looking to dramatically improve their life, their health, and their perspective. David has positively impacted change in the lives of thousands around the country through his guidance and wisdom. Most importantly, he is simply a good man with a great heart and a lot to offer his readers. I am proud to be both a colleague and friend to David Bush and wholeheartedly endorse David's book."

> **DALE VERMILLION**, author, one of the foremost leaders of the mortgage industry, and a highly sought-after international trainer, speaker, and consultant

LIVE AN EXTRAORDINARY LIFE

LIVE AN EXTRAORDINARY LIFE

SIX COMMITMENTS TO LIVE YOUR DREAMS & CHANGE YOUR WORLD

DAVID BUSH

Copyright © 2021 by David Bush

ISBN Softcover: 978-1-7379890-0-4
Ebook ISBN: 978-1-7379890-1-1

All rights reserved. No part of this book may be reproduced or transmitted in any form or by any means, electronic or mechanical, including photocopying, recording, or by any information storage and retrieval system, without permission in writing from the copyright owner. For information on distribution rights, royalties, derivative works, or licensing opportunities on behalf of this content or work, please contact the publisher at the address below.

Printed in the United States of America.

Cover Art: Amanda Anway
Cover and Interior Design: Heidi Caperton

Although the author and publisher have made every effort to ensure that the information and advice in this book was correct and accurate at press time, the author and publisher do not assume and hereby disclaim any liability to any party for any loss, damage, or disruption caused from acting upon the information in this book or by errors or omissions, whether such errors or omissions result from negligence, accident, or any other cause.

eLifePlans LLC
PO Box 191
Pella, IA 50219
www.TheExtraordinaryLife.com

TABLE OF CONTENTS

Foreword. . . . . *xvii*

Introduction 1

Chapter 1: Extraordinary Commitment #1
Live Your Calling. 13

Chapter 2: Extraordinary Commitment #2
Engage in Your Dreams 21

Chapter 3: Extraordinary Commitment #3
Agree to Make Hard Choices 43

Chapter 4: Extraordinary Commitment #4
Decide to Fail Forward 63

Chapter 5: Extraordinary Commitment #5
Expand Your Perspective 81

Chapter 6: Extraordinary Commitment #6
Resolve to Achieve Your Goals 89

Summary 97

LIVE AN EXTRAORDINARY LIFE! 100

Acknowledgments. *101*

About the Author *103*

You can be EXTRAORDINARY and make an EXTRAORDINARY impact in the lives of others!

It is my dream to see your life and the lives of others changed for the better because of this book. If its message inspires, motivates, educates, and challenges you to live an extraordinary life, would you please do me an EXTRAORDINARY favor? Pay it forward by sending your family, friends, clients, customers, and coworkers a link to www.TheExtraordinaryLife.com. Then, share the link on social media with the hashtag #TheExtraordinaryLife so others can benefit from all the free resources available. I appreciate you and all you do to inspire others!

FOREWORD

What makes one extraordinary? The answer is obvious, really; it is those five "extra" letters. Without them, you are left with "ordinary."

David Bush has been my friend and colleague for many years now, and I've seen him go through many of the life challenges and transitions he shares within this empowering book. As your coach, David teaches by guiding you through the processes that cause "extra" payoffs in your life.

He overcame challenges in his physical health, finances, relationships, attitudes toward life, and more. Yet, he learned, changed, and evolved into a man we can all admire.

David's life today is a testimony to the principles and practices laid out for you in this book. He and all the thousands of people he has coached have proven that this is the path to extraordinary living. You can trust this path. It will work for you. I know because I have traveled a similar path so when I say that the lessons in this book will work for you, I mean it!

This is your handbook for transforming your life. Don't be ordinary any longer. Find your EXTRA and follow David Bush's guidance to live an *Extraordinary Life*!

JIM CATHCART,
author of *The Power Minute* and twenty other books, and member of the Professional Speaker Hall of Fame

INTRODUCTION

How would you define what it means to live *an Extraordinary Life?*

Merriam-Webster's Dictionary defines "extraordinary" as *going beyond what is usual, regular, or customary. Exceptional to a very marked extent.*

What is *"usual, regular, or customary"* in our lives is unique to each of us. What is *"exceptional to a very marked extent"* is a matter of opinion. To put it simply, *living an Extraordinary Life* happens when a person clarifies something meaningful to them beyond what is *usual, regular, or customary* and then organizes their life around becoming or doing it. It is when individuals choose to live outside their comfort zone and dare to accomplish something beyond the ordinary. In doing so, they live an *exceptional life to a marked extent.*

We may differ in our definition of what living an *Extraordinary Life* means, and that is okay. What's most important is defining where you are now, what *an Extraordinary Life* means to you, and then creating a plan of action to pursue it with relentless effort and determination, never giving up on your dreams.

From my personal experience and the testimonies of others, living *an Extraordinary Life* is like climbing a mountain, striving to summit new peaks, exploring higher altitudes, and experiencing the amazing views by becoming more, doing more, and/or achieving more in your life.

I have found there are four groups of people with respect to *Extraordinary Life* mountain climbing: one that is actively making the attempt to summit the peak, and three others that for one reason or another, refrain. The image above gives you a visual depiction of each group's position relative to the mountain. Below is a brief description of their attitude toward climbing. Both are intended to help you decide in which group you currently reside.

1. ORDINARY LIFE RIVER RAFTERS

This group is filled with multitudes of people just going with the flow, floating through life, enjoying immediate gratification, pursuing the path of least resistance. They choose not to do anything extraordinary because they either lack knowledge about what's possible or allow fear, doubt, and limiting beliefs to squash faith in their ability to rise above their circumstances and achieve something extraordinary.

Their focus on the here and now keeps them from seeing the benefits of pursuing the extraordinary. Not only that, but the longer they stay in the river, the greater the chance these *River Rafters* will go over the *Waterfall of Life*, a perilous cascade that includes significant failures, regrets, lifestyle-related diseases, relationship issues, and even premature death.

Unfortunately, this group constitutes most of the world's population. Their health, financial statement, education, and life are dictated by their lack of a dream, lack of skills, unhealthy habits, and poor decision-making.

2. VALLEY DWELLERS

This group is filled with complacent people who do not consciously choose either failure or success. They are indecisive and fearful of the consequences of change. They live what they may call the "good life" but often complain about their circumstances. They blame their hardships on others and feel victimized by someone else's choices. They may have a "good" job and average relationships with family and friends. They're not sick but also not healthy. They may have a retirement account, but not one that allows them to live the life they've dreamt about.

Valley Dwellers take short vacations, focus on the cost of everything, and dread going back to work on Mondays after a short weekend of relaxation. They don't love what they do and rarely, if ever, experience the excitement of achieving something truly extraordinary, daring, challenging, or exciting.

These *Valley Dwellers* often lack the thrill of striving for big dreams and something truly EXTRAordinary. They occasionally raft *Ordinary Life River* to bring some immediate gratification and make risky choices, but they descend back into the valley when they begin to experience the pains and consequences associated with their choices just before they go over the *Waterfall of Life*.

Valley Dwellers often stay away from climbing *Extraordinary Life Mountain* because of what their family and friends may think if they choose to strive for something extraordinary. Or, they refrain from doing something extraordinary due to a lack of belief in themselves or lack of a dream, mission, or calling. In doing so, they remain trapped between a failing and *Extraordinary Life*.

3. COMFORT CAVE CAMPERS

People in this group have experienced some level of extraordinary results and success in life but have become comfortable with their achievements. They stopped pursuing the extraordinary and they are living their life focused on past achievements versus challenging themselves to learn more, become more, and achieve more. *Comfort Cave Campers* are filled with talents, gifts, strengths, good health, and the capacity to do so much more to make a huge impact in the world but opt for comfort over significance.

Cave Campers often feel motivated and called to take risks, embrace new challenges, or dream bigger but don't because of the effort, sacrifice, and investment of time and energy required. Or, they fear failure and a potential hit to their ego. When they think about chasing a new dream and climbing a new peak, the motivation passes and remaining comfortable takes priority. This group has the greatest of untapped potential.

4. *EXTRAORDINARY LIFE* CLIFF CLIMBERS

These are the people who live the most extraordinary lives. They constantly strive to reach new peaks of success and significance. They discover and live their calling, realize their dreams, achieve their goals, pioneer new ideas, and create products, experiences, solutions, and businesses to better the lives of others. The world watches this group of leaders live a life filled with adventure, mystery, purpose, and excitement. They turn the impossible into the possible. They show up when others don't. They are often labeled by others as foolish, dreamers, daredevils, or the crazy ones. They are often ridiculed, laughed at, and mocked by the *River Rafters* and *Valley Dwellers* because they don't know what they don't know until they see what they never saw. *Extraordinary Life Cliff Climbers* are remembered long after they die thanks to their heroic efforts, inventions, leadership, and accomplishments.

Being an *Extraordinary Life Cliff Climber* is not for everyone. It is reserved for those who do not accept the status quo and are willing to put in the EXTRA effort, time, sacrifice, and resources to achieve extraordinary results, success, and significance in whatever they feel called to be, do, or have. Becoming an *Extraordinary Life Cliff Climber* is for those who consciously choose to take risks, make sacrifices, and leave lasting legacies for future generations to follow.

"PEOPLE DO NOT DECIDE TO BECOME EXTRAORDINARY. THEY DECIDE TO ACCOMPLISH EXTRAORDINARY THINGS."

- Sir Edmund Hillary, the first person to summit Mount Everest

Sir Edmund Percival Hillary, a New Zealand mountaineer, explorer, and philanthropist, reached the top of Mount Everest, the highest mountain in the world, standing at 29,029 feet, on May 29, 1953. Hillary, who was thirty-three at the time, was accompanied by Nepalese Sherpa mountaineer Tenzing Norgay. The two became the first climbers known to summit Mount Everest and were regarded as the world's preeminent mountaineers.

In an interview following their ascent, Hillary was asked why he decided to climb the mountain. He responded, "I didn't climb the mountain to conquer the mountain. I did it to conquer myself."

Since Hillary and Norgay's ascent, there have been over five thousand successful summit attempts of Everest by climbers worldwide. That means more than five thousand people have conquered themselves because two men decided to do something extraordinary and be the first to reach Mount Everest's peak. This list includes Erik Weihenmayer in 2001 (who is blind), Mark Inglis in 2006 (a double amputee), and Jordan Romero in 2010 (who was only thirteen years old at the time).

When we identify something extraordinary, it becomes the mountain peak we are destined and determined to conquer. Imagine for just a moment how exciting and meaningful your life would be if you chose to pursue an extraordinary calling, mission, dream, or goal that was significant to you, and you conquered it.

Whether you are a *River Rafter, Valley Dweller, Comfort Cave Camper,* or *Cliff Climber* right now does not define your ability to change your life, nor does it define you as a person. What matters most is, do you want to live *an Extraordinary Life,* and are you willing to commit to making it happen? We need more leaders who will no longer accept the ordinary as our everyday reality. We need to grow ourselves into leaders who will live extraordinary lives and deliver extraordinary results.

The opportunity is here for a new American Revolution—a revolution against complacency and the ordinary life. You can choose to answer the call and live an *Extraordinary Life* or ignore it altogether. I believe we all have the power to change the course of events. When enough of us have the same belief, our country (and our lives) will change for the better.

This book reveals the step-by-step strategies and *Six Extraordinary Commitments* that many ordinary people have used to become *Extraordinary Life Cliff Climbers* and live successful, fulfilled, extraordinary lives.

SIX EXTRAORDINARY COMMITMENTS

RESOLVE TO ACHIEVE YOUR GOALS

EXPAND YOUR PERSPECTIVE

DECIDE TO FAIL FORWARD

AGREE TO MAKE HARD CHOICES

ENGAGE IN YOUR DREAMS

LIVE YOUR CALLING

I'll provide the insights I've used and coached thousands of others to use to give you the motivation and skills needed to design and live your own *Extraordinary Life.* If you commit to investing the time to adopt the extraordinary habits and skills, your results will be staggering!

BY READING THIS BOOK, YOU WILL...

- Learn the secrets found in every *Extraordinary Life Cliff Climber* and how to replicate their success in your life.
- Understand why we are all called to live *An Extraordinary Life.*
- Discover real-life stories of how ordinary people created extraordinary lives.

BY TAKING THE SPECIAL INTERACTIVE CHALLENGE IN THIS BOOK, YOU WILL...

- Regain focus on your highest priorities and improve your overall life balance.
- Get a firm sense of direction of what you need to do to maximize your opportunities and potential.
- Break through obstacles and challenges to achieve extraordinary results in every aspect of your life.

WHERE ARE YOU?

Are you a *Cliff Climber, Cave Camper, Valley Dweller,* or *River Rafter* who's headed for the falls of Ordinary Life River? Complete this *Extraordinary Life* Assessment and let's explore where you are now so we can determine where you can go. (*NOTE: Download a copy of this assessment at TheExtraordinaryLife.com*)

Complete the assessment by assigning a value 1 to 10 (10 being the best you could possibly do) in each of the following areas:

PHYSICAL WELL-BEING

Healthy weight

Nutrition Habits (eating a balanced nutrition plan with healthy foods)

Hydration Habits (drinking 80 oz. of water daily)

Energy Management (sleeping well, energized, and rested)

Fitness Habits (exercising regularly, staying active for
30 minutes or more daily)

No medications (for lifestyle-related diseases)

Physical Well-Being Score: (add all the above scores here)

MENTAL WELL-BEING

Handle stress well

Time for family and friends

Happy and fulfilled

Enjoying career (or retirement)

Spiritually healthy

Pursuing hobbies and other interests

Mental Well-Being Score: (add all the above scores here)

FINANCIAL/VOCATIONAL WELL-BEING

Enjoying career/business and work environment

Debt free

Savings for emergencies

Retirement fund

Abundance of time and money to contribute to worthy causes

Fun cash for vacations, hobbies, entertainment

Financial Well-Being Total Score: (add all the above scores here)

COMBINED TOTAL SCORE FROM ALL THREE CATEGORIES:

(physical/mental/financial)

HOW DID YOU SCORE?

>151=
EXTRAORDINARY LIFE
CLIFF CLIMBERS

121-150 =
COMFORT CAVE
CAMPERS

91-120 =
VALLEY OF
COMPLACENCEY
DWELLERS

61-90 =
ORDINARY LIFE
RIVER RAFTERS

ORDINARY LIFE
RIVER FALLS

<60 =
FAILING

Now that you know where you are currently, let me guide you to clarify the peak of your own *Extraordinary Life* mountain and guide you through the six extraordinary commitments and action steps you will need to take on to conquer your own *Extraordinary Life* mountain.

CHAPTER 1

EXTRAORDINARY COMMITMENT #1
LIVE YOUR CALLING

History has proven *Extraordinary Life Cliff Climbers* come in all colors, shapes, and sizes. Yet, they share common commitments, the first of which is to **LIVE YOUR CALLING**.

Every great leader answers a call in their life. Some *Cliff Climbers* respond to a call from another leader who called them to be or do something extraordinary, and others to an inner calling that challenged them to follow their heart and go beyond the status quo.

Cliff Climbers choose to live their calling day after day, week after week, month after month, and year after year. That is how a remarkable legacy is achieved.

Unfortunately, many people want to live an *Extraordinary Life* but have a list of reasons why they can't: fear, doubt, uncertainty, busyness, insufficient finances, lack of support or time. They *decide* not to take the time to identify their true calling and become comfortable with ordinary lives as *River Rafters, Valley Dwellers,* or *Cave Campers.*

Bronnie Ware, an Australian nurse who spent several years working in palliative care tending to patients in the last twelve weeks of their lives, recorded their dying epiphanies in her book, *The Top Five Regrets of the Dying.* I believe her findings give us great perspective on our future if we fail to clarify and live our calling. Here are the top five regrets as witnessed by Ware:

1. I wish I'd had the courage to live a life true to myself, not the life others expected of me.
"This was the most common regret of all. When people realize that their life is almost over and look back clearly on it, it is easy to see how many dreams have gone unfulfilled. Most people had not honored even a half of their dreams and had to die knowing that it was due to choices they had made, or not made. Health brings a freedom very few realize, until they no longer have it."

2. I wish I hadn't worked so hard.
"This came from every male patient that I nursed. They missed their children's youth and their partner's companionship. Women also spoke of this regret, but as most were from an older generation, many of the female patients had not been breadwinners. All of the men I nursed deeply regretted spending so much of their lives on the treadmill of a work existence."

3. I wish I'd had the courage to express my feelings.
"Many people suppressed their feelings in order to keep peace with others. As a result, they settled for a mediocre existence and never became who they were truly capable of becoming. Many developed illnesses relating to the bitterness and resentment they carried as a result."

4. I wish I had stayed in touch with my friends.
"Often, they would not truly realize the full benefits of old friends until their dying weeks, and it was not always possible to track them down. Many had become so caught up in their own lives that they had let golden friendships slip by over the years. There were many deep regrets about not giving friendships the time and effort that they deserved. Everyone misses their friends when they are dying."

5. I wish that I had let myself be happier.
"This is a surprisingly common one. Many did not realize until the end that happiness is a choice. They had stayed stuck in old patterns and habits. The so-called 'comfort' of familiarity overflowed into their emotions, as well as their physical lives. Fear of change had them pretending to others, and to themselves, that they were content, when deep within, they longed to laugh properly and have silliness in their life again."

AN EXTRAORDINARY QUESTION:

If you were to die today, would you have any of the same regrets listed above?

Are you ready to clarify and *Live Your Calling*? If your answer is yes, read on!

ANSWERING THE CALL TO LIVE AN *EXTRAORDINARY LIFE*

I grew up in a middle-class, self-employed family. My dad owned an auto body shop and my mom helped in the office while raising my brother Jeff and me. They worked hard and were extraordinary dreamers who epitomized what it meant to be *Extraordinary Life Cliff Climbers*. They believed anything was possible, took risks, chased the *American Dream,* and ran a successful small business. They believed in an *Extraordinary Life* and reminded us that nothing truly great happens without sacrifice and hard work.

My parents would listen to personal growth audio cassettes in the car, and those messages called us to a greater purpose. Top personal and professional development leaders, such as Zig Ziglar, Denis Waitley, and Jim Rohn, were passengers in our car, sharing their world-changing philosophies and ideas. My parents also watched public television specials and TV shows that featured prominent motivational speakers, like Les Brown, and passionate pastors, like Dr. Robert Schuller, who consistently spoke words of truth, hope, and inspiration into our lives.

As a kid, I felt a calling to one day become a motivational speaker and Peak Performance Coach — someone who assisted and encouraged others to live out their calling, and who motivated them to **reach** their full potential. However, at the time, I was not prepared to live out my calling. Like a *River Rafter*, my social circle was focused on the immediate gratifications in life. My own limiting beliefs and self-doubts prevented me from responding positively and proactively to my calling. I wasn't ready to make the changes needed, nor was I willing to give the **extra** effort required to make it happen.

I've learned many people experience this over the years. Many of us have put the pillow over our ears when we hear the calling or experience a wake-up call. We avoid it out of fear of the unknown, limiting beliefs, fatigue, or lack of energy. We crave the comfort of rafting the ordinary life river. We are unsure if the calling—climbing the path of resistance and risking failure—is worth the effort.

Unfortunately, some people have never been called to be or do something by an influencer in their life, nor were they recognized for their unique talents, skills, and gifts. They grew up in homes where powerful influencers discouraged them from answering the call. Some were trained to unplug an *Extraordinary Life* alarm clock, so the calling wasn't heard, or if it was, family and friends mocked and ridiculed their "cliff climbing" desires because of their lack of understanding, education, or personal experiences.

Others have listened to this wake-up call ring in their head day in and day out. They have been trying to answer but struggled for various reasons. They may have lacked the motivation, mindset, skillsets and action required. The calling is there, but nobody has helped them to clarify it or grow their confidence in answering it.

I believe each one of us has a calling and a greater purpose in life. I think everyone can live an *Extraordinary Life* if they answer the call and wake up to the benefits of doing so. My goal is to help you live your calling, but only if you are interested and willing to do the work, regardless of your circumstances. If you are ready to begin exploring what it means to live an *Extraordinary Life*, let's clarify what you feel called to be, do, or have by completing the exercise below.

EXTRAORDINARY LIFE ACTION STEP: CLARIFY YOUR CALLING

What do you (or your family and friends) believe are your three greatest strengths, talents, gifts, or qualities?

What specific activities bring you the most joy and fulfillment?

If time and money were not an issue, what would you give back or contribute to your family, friends, community, schools, place of worship, country, or the world?

For which group of people are you most naturally concerned (e.g., kids, single moms, those who are unhealthy, needy, poor, addicted, abused, etc.)? What breaks your heart? Who do you want to help?

What would you like the epitaph on your gravestone to read?

What type of legacy would you like to leave after you die? (What do you want to be remembered for?)

What are your answers to these questions showing you?

Where do you see a calling in your life? How could your talents, skills, and gifts be leveraged to fulfill your calling?

Why do you think you exist here on Earth? What do you sense you are called to do or be?

CHAPTER 2

EXTRAORDINARY COMMITMENT #2
ENGAGE IN YOUR DREAMS

Most of history's *Extraordinary Life Cliff Climbers* started out as ordinary people with ordinary backgrounds, educations, and upbringings. However, something triggered a transformation that allowed them to change an ordinary life into an extraordinary one. This transformation began the day they integrated a particular catalyst into their life.

Merriam-Webster's Dictionary defines a catalyst as "an agent that provokes or speeds up significant change." In this case, the catalyst I'm talking about is a dream that turns a calling into a vision of something you want to be, do, and/or have. A calling can be an unmeasurable mission. A dream is more of a specific vision of something you desire that is congruent with your life's calling or mission.

Henry David Thoreau said, "If one advances confidently in the direction of his dreams, and endeavors to live the life which he has imagined, he will meet with a success unexpected in common hours."

One of the greatest gifts we have in life is the ability to dream—not just any kind of dream, but the dreams that change us and shape the world we live in. It requires the ability to dream of things that never were and then turn them into tangible realities. The right dreams can transform our world, capture our imagination, and engage all our senses and energies, inspiring us to pursue an extraordinary dream day after day.

I have chosen to use the word *catalyst* to describe this process because the dream I am talking about is not a fantasy. A catalyst dream has a practical effect: it speeds up the delivery of a predictable and significant change in your life and the lives of those around you.

Every *Cliff Climber* in history who's lived an *Extraordinary Life* has had a dream or vision—a unique catalyst, which transformed that person's life. Each of these leaders' catalysts was special, and yours is too. If you want to live an *Extraordinary Life*, you must spend the time necessary to identify your dreams to engage the catalyst that energizes you and speeds up positive life change.

A good catalyst wakes you up early and keeps you up late, encouraging you to hike uphill toward it. It moves you forward in your vision regardless of the obstacles you face because when the dream is big enough, the facts do not count! Your catalyst must inspire you to daily action.

Read what two of the world's most *Extraordinary Life Cliff Climbers* said about the catalyst:

"What man actually needs is not a tensionless state but rather the striving and struggling for some goal worthy of him. What he needs is not the discharge of tension at any cost, but the call of a potential

meaning waiting to be fulfilled by him." – Victor Frankl, Austrian neurologist and Holocaust survivor

"*When you discover your mission, you will feel its demand. It will fill you with enthusiasm and a burning desire to get to work on it.*" – W. Clement Stone, American businessman and philanthropist

Extraordinary dreams and visions spark a change in you. They inspire you to pursue not just any action but those that connect you with who you were truly meant to be. These visionary undertakings become like a giant magnet pulling you through all the challenges and obstacles standing before you.

As you're pulled through, you discover who you were really meant to be in this life. You might find you are meant to:

- Achieve something significant and/or remarkable in your field, family, or community.
- Own a successful business and deliver a valuable product and/or service to improve the lives of others.
- Invent a cure or answer to a unique challenge to make a difference in the lives of others.
- Change the world forever through your sincere willingness to act on a vision inside your heart and mind.

I do not know whether any of those dreams constitute your catalyst, but I do believe if you are not 100 percent clear on what yours is, you should be looking for it daily if you want to live an *Extraordinary Life.* You may not feel confident that you can live an *Extraordinary Life.* This idea may seem too lofty, but realizing just one dream can grow your confidence and competence. Your dream may just be the highest peak on the mountain you can see, not the actual mountain summit. Realizing one dream may just give you a peek at your next peak but your catalyst, the thing that truly energizes you, is waiting for you to find it—and the world around you is depending on you to apply it to your life.

Remember how you used to dream as a child? Fear didn't stop you from dreaming of achieving extraordinary ideas. Look once again for the same sense of wonder, possibility, and complete, unshakeable dedication. When you find a dream "hardwired" into your answer to the question, "What's most important to me?", take note. You have found a clue to your catalyst.

To find this dream, simply ask yourself the same question grown-ups used to ask endlessly when you were a kid: What do you want to be, do, or have when you grow up? When the answer is something you feel strong, positive emotion about, something you will want to come back to again and again, you can begin the process of achieving it.

"THE MORE INTENSELY WE FEEL ABOUT AN IDEA OR A GOAL, THE MORE ASSUREDLY THE IDEA, BURIED DEEP IN OUR SUBCONSCIOUS, WILL DIRECT US ALONG THE PATH TO ITS FULFILLMENT."

- Earl Nightingale

Find your catalyst and act on it. When you identify your catalyst, you change your world. When you change your world, you live an *Extraordinary Life*! The time is now!

MY FIRST EXPERIENCE WITH DREAMING

My grandfather Henry Alldis was a standout running back from Northern California who went to the University of Southern California (USC) to play football. He was legendary in our family, but I never got a chance to meet him because he died of a heart attack at age forty-seven while working as a security guard at a Los Angeles Rams football game in the Los Angeles Coliseum — the same stadium where he played college football. He was a teacher, husband to my grandmother Dorothy, and father to four kids. My mom was only sixteen years old at the time.

I grew up as a big, heavy kid, usually the biggest on the playground. I honestly did not like being the biggest because it came with many fat jokes at my expense. My position in sports was usually dictated by my size, not my personal interests. I played catcher in baseball, goalie in soccer, and lineman in football. I was an ordinary athlete in most sports, but football was where I showed the greatest promise.

Growing up, many of my family members would tell me I looked like my grandfather. Because of some God-given athletic talent, strength, and skills, I thrived on the football field from a very young age, receiving positive reinforcement by the coaches and other players. This experience led me to dream of becoming a successful college and professional football player, and turn a negative (my size) into a positive.

I became one of the star players on the football team in my small high school and started to see the benefits of answering the call to become the best I could be. I began the *extaordinary* process of elevating my motivation, mindset, skillset, and activities to change my future and see how far I could go to make my football dreams come true.

In the off-season of my junior year in high school, I began working with a personal trainer to enhance my physical strength, agility, and speed. It paid off in my senior season. We became the conference champions, and I was named the Most Valuable Player of the Freedom Conference. This was my first experience being recognized as a *Cliff Climber* in my field. I liked how I felt and was proud of what I had accomplished. This gave me the confidence to believe in my dream and press on.

However, while I felt a calling to play football at the collegiate level, I did not get any calls from major universities that I had dreamed about. I hoped to fulfill my grandfather's legacy at the University of Southern California, but my dream quickly turned into a nightmare when no one recruited me to play college football for that school—or any other school for that matter.

Rather than give up, I chose to continue pursuing my dream. I enrolled at Orange Coast Community College in Costa Mesa, California, and became an All-Conference Offensive Center. I was offered a scholarship to the University of South Dakota (USD). I joked with my family that I was just one consonant off from USC! However, the difference turned out to be seventeen hundred miles away from my Southern California home.

By pursuing my passion and dream of becoming a successful football player, I was recognized as an All-Conference and All-American Offensive Center and Long Snapper for punts and field goals at the USD. I felt like I had worked hard and realized my college dreams despite not attending USC.

Then, I decided to pursue my dream of playing professional football. There was just one problem: no professional football teams were calling to recruit me. Once again, I had to continue believing in myself and my talents, skills, and abilities even when other people did not.

Unfortunately, not having an agent to represent me, I had to seek mentorship and expertise to learn what it would take to become a professional football player. I had some significant influences in my life who encouraged me to craft a plan to achieve my dream and organize my life around it. In doing so, I prioritized the habits of professional football players. I posted the plan on the ceiling above my bed so I would see it every morning when I wanted to sleep in or take a nap. There were some mornings I would lay in bed with my eyes closed, and this extraordinary plan would be staring at me, saying, "Get up!" It became the catalyst that provoked me to act and do the work to make it happen.

I made a list of every team in the National Football League, Canadian Football League, World Football League, and Arena Football League—the four leagues that paid players. I called each one and sent them a copy of a highlight videotape I created from my football games.

Sending the videotapes was not easy, but it was easier than following up with each person who received them. Most of the time I heard nothing in response, so I called over and over until I could talk to someone. It was extremely challenging mentally and emotionally to overcome my self-doubt and discouragement from not hearing positive feedback in the process of pursuing my dream and selling myself to others. But because I had a motivating dream, I tackled uncomfortable and demanding tasks.

I finally got a call back from a team in New York, the Albany Firebirds of the Arena Football League. They were the first to offer me a chance to try out, but it came with a challenge. I had to pay my own way to get to their facility, and being a recent college graduate, I did not have much money.

My family had given me a small sum for graduation, so I decided to invest all of it into a plane ticket to Albany, New York. When I arrived at the airport, I was met by a large, very intimidating-looking man. His name was Jerome. He had graduated from one of the best football schools in the US. He was taller than me and his body was chiseled. On the way to the practice facility, I silently prayed that the other players competing for my position did not look like Jerome!

I discovered quickly how professional football brings the best, biggest, and fastest players together to create high-performance teams, regardless of the league. The night before my tryout, I began to doubt myself and whether I was good enough to compete at this level. While I showed up at the tryout physically, I did not show up mentally. I was humiliated by the veteran players and failed to perform to my full potential.

At the end of the tryout, one of the coaches came up to me and told me that while I was a good college player, I was not good enough to play professional football. I walked off the field feeling crushed, defeated, and disappointed. I felt like a failure, that my dream of playing professionally had come to an end. I reached a point where I had to decide to really go after my dream and believe in myself or be satisfied with living an ordinary life.

When I returned to my home at the USD, I learned I had received an offer to become a graduate assistant to the football team. They would pay for me to get my master's degree as part of a football scholarship. It was an excellent opportunity but not the dream I had long hoped for—it was a safe *Plan B.*

I wasn't ready to give up on my dream of playing professional football, so I made one of the most pivotal decisions in my life: I decided to go ALL IN. I went into extreme *Cliff Climber* mode and packed ALL my earthly belongings into the bed of my pickup truck, rented out my room, gave notice to the school and team that I wouldn't be taking their offer, and left campus to pursue my dream. I decided to drive to every professional football team and ask if I could try out. I was sick to my stomach, filled with fear, but felt fully alive as I embarked on my adventure. I was ALL IN.

I made a fundamental shift in my mindset. I would not let my dream pass by or permit my past *River Rafter, Valley Dweller,* and *Cave Camper* limiting beliefs, self-doubt, and concerns stop me from doing something I dreamt of since I was a little kid.

In June of 1995, I showed up in Des Moines, Iowa, where an arena football team called the Iowa Barnstormers was based. They were in their first season of play, and they were about six games into the regular season. The owner, Jim Foster, was the creator of Arena Football. The Barnstormers had an all-star roster of players from top universities, including many from the National Football League, World Football League, and Canadian Football League.

They offered me an opportunity to try out, and I did not disappoint. I was ALL IN and had no better alternatives than to play for their team at that point in time. My new attitude and mindset allowed me to perform at a much higher level—a level I was fully capable of in Albany — I just needed a different motivation.

During the tryout, I threw a couple of three-hundred-plus pound men to the ground and, in doing so, caught the coach's attention. When the practice was over, the coach told me they were really impressed with my performance but that right now, they didn't need anyone because they had a full roster. However, he said they would call me when they were ready. I was disappointed but had a new degree of belief and self-confidence.

One of my mentors told me that if a professional football team expresses interest, don't leave that opportunity! So, I made another pivotal decision that day—I offered to practice with the team for free. I remember the surprise on the head coach John Gregory's face. He responded, "You'd do that? You'd have to sign a liability waiver, which would mean if you got hurt, you would be fully responsible for any medical costs associated with your injuries because we can't formally sign you to the team."

I agreed and signed the waiver. I was ALL IN. Living out your dreams in pursuit of an *Extraordinary Life* requires taking risks, and this was one of the biggest I had ever taken. Because I was willing to take it, though, I stood out as an EXTRAordinary teammate even if I was not the fastest, strongest, or most talented player available. It was likely one of the major reasons they accepted my offer and expressed increased interest in me.

I got a part-time job at Office Depot and showed up for practice the following day. I remember the other players asking me why I was there if I was not on the team. I told them I was just helping prepare the team and myself if I was needed. Some of them laughed and poked fun; others were impressed with my conviction.

I have found in living an *Extraordinary Life*, there will always be laughers, mockers, and believers! We need to tune out the laughers and mockers and tune in to those who believe in us.

After two weeks of practicing with the team for no pay, both of the guys who played my position suffered an injury. I remember it like it was yesterday: I signed my first professional football contract with the Iowa Barnstormers. Even though it was not the NFL, I felt like I had accomplished something extraordinary. I had gone above and beyond the usual, regular, and customary and was rewarded with an opportunity to do something very few people ever get to do. They say the odds of getting to play professional football are like the same as being struck by lightning twice! I felt a huge sense of accomplishment that day.

Once I knew what I was capable of, I continued to pursue professional football at the highest level with the NFL and attended many tryouts with professional scouts. I did not find a team that would sign me, but I did play four seasons with the Iowa Barnstormers and got an opportunity to develop close friendships with many great people.

Our team played in two World Championship games, and some of my teammates went on to dominate in the NFL. Kurt Warner, our quarterback, was one of them. Kurt became a member of the Professional Football Hall of Fame in Canton, Ohio. During the induction ceremony, he even thanked a few other players and me for helping him succeed, which, to me, was extraordinary!

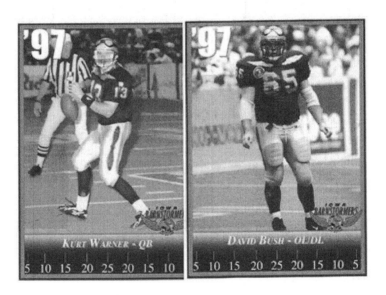

I continue to kid Kurt that without me hiking him the ball, he would never have been MVP of the Arena Football League, a Super Bowl champion quarterback, an NFL MVP award winner, or Hall of Famer, so he is on the hook for the tab whenever we connect!

In all seriousness, I discovered that pursuing an extraordinary dream does not always end with you realizing that dream. However, the person you become in its pursuit is greater than the dream itself. There is also an extraordinary ripple effect in your life and the lives of others because of your decisions and actions.

Once you overcome fear and adversity, and start to sacrifice to accomplish something extraordinary, you see the rewards, begin to understand what is possible, and dream bigger. Then, you can replicate that same process in pursuit of other dreams to live an *Extraordinary Life*.

Now, let's talk about your dreams. I want to help you get clear on what matters most to you!

EXTRAORDINARY LIFE ACTION STEP: DEFINE YOUR EXTRAORDINARY DREAMS

IF YOU DON'T DESIGN YOUR OWN LIFE PLAN, CHANCES ARE YOU'LL FALL INTO SOMEONE ELSE'S PLAN. AND GUESS WHAT THEY HAVE PLANNED FOR YOU? NOT MUCH!

- Jim Rohn, American business philosopher

Clarifying your dreams and defining what you want to be, do, and have can be a challenging exercise for some. Focus is an essential element. *Merriam-Webster's Dictionary* defines the word *focus* as "the center of activity, attraction, or attention. A point of concentration."

Are you focused on a point of concentration in your life? Until we become intentional about achieving this type of clarity, we will feel lost; we will not have a clear understanding of where we are going.

When we were children, focusing on our dreams may have been much easier. We could dream about our future without the fear, doubt, and negative influences we may have now or the pain of past failures that often keep us from trying something again or something new. However, with just a little practice and a growth mindset, we can reclaim that childlike focus whenever we choose!

For the next few minutes, I want you to think about getting into a helicopter to take an aerial view of your entire life. What do you see as you look down on your career, relationships, finances, and health? What is happening as you look at your life from five thousand feet?

BEGIN DREAMING ABOUT YOUR *EXTRAORDINARY LIFE!*

Download a copy of this dreaming exercise at
TheExtraordinaryLife.com.

What would you like to see happen during your lifetime? What do you see yourself achieving? What do you intend to do "in your life" and "with your life"? What kind of impact would you like to make because of your life? Dream about the possibilities and don't worry if it sounds impossible based on your current circumstances.

PHYSICAL WELL-BEING

What would you like to lose, gain, quit, or start doing consistently with your physical health?

What would you like to be, do, or have with your physical health and fitness level?

Goal weight _____ lbs.
Get to ___% body fat
Wear a size ____

Other Physical Dreams:
☐ Run or walk a 5k or 10k race.
☐ Run a half-marathon, marathon, or triathlon.
☐ _____
☐ _____

CAREER/BUSINESS/FINANCIAL WELL-BEING

What would you like to be (business owner, position, or title), do (responsibilities), and have (specifically)? What would your ideal business/career look like if you could do anything?

What amount of monthly income would make you smile?

What amount of monthly income would blow your mind?

If money weren't an issue, what would you splurge on?

Do you want to retire from working altogether? If so, when?

MENTAL WELL-BEING

What relationships would you like to start, improve, or eliminate?

Who do you want to spend more time with?

What would bring you more peace of mind, purpose, and fulfillment?

What do you want to learn, become, and understand at a deeper level?

DO YOU WANT TO ADD ANY OF THESE ADVENTURES TO YOUR LIFE?
(Check the box of each activity you would like to experience)

- ☐ Learn a new language
- ☐ Learn to play an instrument
- ☐ See a Broadway play
- ☐ Go zip-lining
- ☐ Learn to dance
- ☐ Go backpacking
- ☐ Start your own business
- ☐ Write a book
- ☐ Ride a motorcycle
- ☐ Go snowmobiling
- ☐ Play paintball
- ☐ Go hang gliding
- ☐ Ride in a helicopter

- ☐ Go whitewater rafting
- ☐ Fly first-class
- ☐ Ride in a hot air balloon
- ☐ Play in a waterfall
- ☐ Be part of a flash mob
- ☐ Drive Route 66
- ☐ Go cliff jumping
- ☐ Go ice skating
- ☐ Go indoor skydiving
- ☐ Go Jet-skiing
- ☐ Go kitesurfing or kiteboarding
- ☐ Go on a road trip with a friend

- [ ] Go camping
- [ ] Go mountain biking
- [ ] Go paragliding
- [ ] Go sand surfing
- [ ] Go waterskiing
- [ ] Go windsurfing
- [ ] Plant a tree
- [ ] Sleep underneath the stars
- [ ] Solve a Rubik's Cube
- [ ] Watch a meteor shower
- [ ] Climb a rock wall
- [ ] Drive a dune buggy
- [ ] Go skydiving
- [ ] Go SCUBA diving
- [ ] Go bungee jumping
- [ ] Ride a Segway, horse, camel, elephant
- [ ] Swim with dolphins/ whales/sharks
- [ ] Race cars on a track
- [ ] Go to a rodeo
- [ ] Watch a TV show live
- [ ] Climb a mountain
- [ ] Go to a TED conference
- [ ] Go on a major cruise
- [ ] Go racing at Talladega

- [ ] Go to the World Series
- [ ] Go to the Super Bowl
- [ ] Go to an Olympics Opening Ceremony
- [ ] Go to Olympics events live
- [ ] Go to a PGA Tour event
- [ ] Attend a Kentucky Derby
- [ ] Get an autograph and picture with (name of celebrity or athlete)

_____

- [ ] See a Vegas show
- [ ] Watch a [artist or band name] concert live
- [ ] See one game at every baseball stadium
- [ ] See one game at every football stadium
- [ ] See one game at every (sport) stadium

_____

- [ ] Watch a Wimbledon championship match
- [ ] Watch a WWE match live
- [ ] Watch an NBA All-Star Weekend live

- ☐ Watch the world's best fireworks displays
- ☐ Watch an exhibition by the US Air Force Thunderbirds
- ☐ Watch an opera
- ☐ Watch a world-class symphony orchestra perform
- ☐ Watch a live ballet performance of *Swan Lake*
- ☐ Watch all of [film director's name] films
- ☐ _____
- ☐ Learn how to play [name of sports]
- ☐ _____
- ☐ Learn archery
- ☐ Learn how to play chess
- ☐ Learn how to snowboard
- ☐ Learn how to ice-skate
- ☐ Learn to ski
- ☐ Learn to surf
- ☐ Learn Taekwondo/Aikido/ Jujitsu/Karate

- ☐ Learn how to cook [name of dish]
- ☐ _____
- ☐ Learn how to bake [name of cake or pastry]
- ☐ _____
- ☐ Learn how to speak [name of languages]
- ☐ _____
- ☐ Learn how to play [name of games]
- ☐ _____
- ☐ Learn how to play poker
- ☐ Learn how to ride a horse
- ☐ Learn how to ride a motorcycle
- ☐ Learn how to shoot a gun
- ☐ Increase your photography skills
- ☐ Learn sign language
- ☐ Learn to juggle
- ☐ Learn to knit or sew
- ☐ Learn to speed read
- ☐ Learn how to cross-stitch
- ☐ Learn how to play guitar

- [ ] Learn public speaking
- [ ] Learn how to meditate
- [ ] Learn self-defense
- [ ] Learn how to budget
- [ ] Become an expert in [name of field or industry]

- [ ] Learn at least ____ magic tricks
- [ ] Learn how to blow glass
- [ ] Learn how to practice mindfulness
- [ ] Learn how to make a sculpture
- [ ] Get married
- [ ] Become a parent
- [ ] Adopt and raise a child
- [ ] Be a bridesmaid/ groomsman
- [ ] Get a bachelor's or master's degree or PhD
- [ ] Become debt-free
- [ ] Buy an investment property
- [ ] Buy a brand-new car
- [ ] Become a millionaire by [age] _____

- [ ] Live and/or study abroad for [time period]

_____

- [ ] Join a specific ministry in church

_____

PLACES TO VISIT:

(Check the states you would like to visit or experience and list the countries)

☐ Alabama	☐ Maine	☐ Oregon
☐ Alaska	☐ Maryland	☐ Pennsylvania
☐ Arizona	☐ Massachusetts	☐ Rhode Island
☐ Arkansas	☐ Michigan	☐ South Carolina
☐ California	☐ Minnesota	☐ South Dakota
☐ Colorado	☐ Mississippi	☐ Tennessee
☐ Connecticut	☐ Missouri	☐ Texas
☐ Delaware	☐ Montana	☐ Utah
☐ Florida	☐ Nebraska	☐ Vermont
☐ Georgia	☐ Nevada	☐ Virginia
☐ Hawaii	☐ New Hampshire	☐ Washington
☐ Idaho	☐ New Jersey	☐ West Virginia
☐ Illinois	☐ New Mexico	☐ Wisconsin
☐ Indiana	☐ New York	☐ Wyoming
☐ Iowa	☐ North Carolina	
☐ Kansas	☐ North Dakota	
☐ Kentucky	☐ Ohio	
☐ Louisiana	☐ Oklahoma	

COUNTRIES TO VISIT:

_____   _____

_____   _____

_____   _____

_____   _____

_____   _____

There is no balance in life without knowing your priorities. An ancient proverb says, "Where your treasure is, there your heart will be also." Truer words have never been spoken. Prioritizing is simply a matter of asking: What do you treasure?

Spell out the word *treasure* vertically and write the answer to each of the following questions to the right of the letter.

T – Where do you spend the most time?

R – Where do you invest the most resources?

E - Where do you invest most of your energy?

A – Where do you dedicate your abilities?

S – What occupies the most space in your life?

U – What fills your utterances?

R – What do you do for recreation?

E – What are you most eager to do?

WHERE YOUR HEART IS . . . PRIORITIZE! If you do not like the way your life is currently prioritized, do not worry. You can change it quickly and see the benefits almost immediately.

PRIORITIZING YOUR DREAMS

Important questions to answer...

- What dreams are the most valuable to me?
- What needs my full attention right now?
- What must I accomplish first?
- How many hours, days, or months will this take to finish, and is it dependent on others?
- Who can help me make these dreams a reality?
- How much money will be required to achieve this dream?
- What do I NEED to accomplish before I can do what I really WANT to do?

Once you have reflected on these questions, go back and write the letter A, B, C, or D next to each dream based on how important realizing that dream is to you.

A – Very important and urgent
B – Very important but not urgent
C – Not very important but urgent
D – Not very important and not urgent

Then prioritize each dream you identified with a number (1 = most important, i.e., A1, A2, B1, B2, C1, C2, D1, D2) so you have a prioritized list of all your dreams. After that, proceed to the next chapter to create your *Extraordinary Life* Plan to help you act on your dreams!

THE KEY IS NOT TO PRIORITIZE WHAT'S ON YOUR SCHEDULE, BUT TO SCHEDULE YOUR PRIORITIES.

– Stephen R. Covey, Best-Selling Author

BONUS EXERCISE @ THEEXTRAORDINARYLIFE.COM:

Watch the free webinar on "Building Your Vision Board"

CHAPTER 3

EXTRAORDINARY COMMITMENT #3
AGREE TO MAKE HARD CHOICES

"WE ALL MUST TRY TO BE THE BEST PERSON WE CAN: BY MAKING THE BEST CHOICES, BY MAKING THE MOST OF THE TALENTS WE'VE BEEN GIVEN."

- Mary Lou Retton, Olympic gold medalist

By now, you should know your world is the sum of the choices you make. An *Extraordinary Life* is reserved for *Cliff Climbers* who are willing to make conscious (and sometimes daring) choices about the life they want to live. The better we get at making these, the better we will get at acting and producing positive results supporting our options.

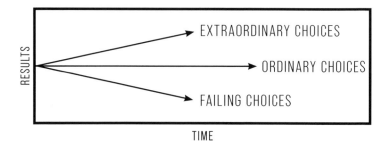

The image below may be a more realistic look at a person's life. There are constant changes taking place because of our decisions or lack thereof. We don't just regret the choices we make that lead to failure or ordinary results, we can also lament those we fail to make.

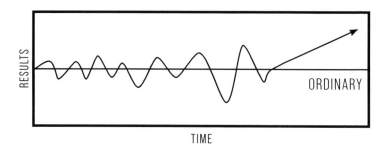

REALITY CHECK: Wanting to live an *Extraordinary Life* and doing so starts with your commitments and choosing to do HARD things. Most people will say they want to live an *Extraordinary Life* but fail because of their choices and lack of commitment. They settle on *Cave Camping, Valley Dwelling,* or *River Rafting* instead.

WHAT'S IN YOUR BACKPACK?

Our minds are filled with experiences. Like a climber's backpack, our minds store things for future use. Others have put thoughts, beliefs, and perspectives inside our backpack from the time we were born. To live an *Extraordinary Life*, leaders need to review what's in their backpack and clean it up with positive ideas, thoughts, beliefs, and skills. Otherwise, whatever they're carrying from the past will begin to weigh them down and prevent them from climbing. The choices we make daily determine what goes into the backpack, what gets used daily, and what gets thrown out.

Bad choices and decisions need to be corrected. It can be scary to go back and look at outdated assumptions and old ways of viewing life or ourselves based on our past choices. But the heavy thoughts we are carrying in our backpacks that are holding us back and weighing us down really have to go, and the only way we're going to get rid of them is by making better choices.

Yes, making a life change and cleaning out your "backpack" of all the useless thoughts, limiting beliefs, and wasteful concepts can be hard. But making the tough choices means you are going beyond what is usual, regular, or customary. This is what *Extraordinary Life Cliff Climbers* do!

As you start going through your backpack, you will have to get clear about what exactly keeps you from going beyond what is usual, regular, or customary.

- Is it fear?
- Is it the lack of self-confidence or a limiting belief?
- Is it an unhealthy habit you have tried to change in the past but failed to do so?
- Is it an unhealthy relationship you are involved in?
- Is it the uncertainty of how others may react if you say or do something different?
- Is it an experience you have not yet processed and moved beyond?

To live an *Extraordinary Life*, you must get rid of the old, heavy stuff in your backpack so you can put in the good stuff needed for your ascent to the summit. You must make room for your dreams and goals and know the bad can ruin the good if you allow it to remain.

Even if you don't consciously choose to make a positive change in some area of your life, you have still made a choice. You've chosen to keep something heavy in your backpack. You've chosen to let it weigh you down. You will begin to regret the decisions you've made (or failed to make) along the way, and you'll suffer the consequences of your actions (or inaction).

"IF WE DID THE THINGS WE ARE CAPABLE OF, WE WOULD ASTOUND OURSELVES."

- Thomas Edison

Think about the catalyst in your own life. What choice could you make right now that would help you bring this dream into reality? Your life clock is ticking! Make a conscious choice to live every day as if it were your last. Then, one day, sooner than you expect, you will be right!

Below, I've listed some *Extraordinary Life Cliff Climbers* who started as ordinary people, just like you and I did when we were born. Each of these leaders made choices that moved them toward the things they wanted to be, do, and have in life.

They refined the skill of making great choices to improve their ability to master new habits to pursue their dream(s). Their ability to create extraordinary decisions every day turned their ordinary lives into extraordinary legends of history.

ELON MUSK (ENGINEER)	Born on June 28, 1971, in Pretoria, South Africa. As a child, Musk was so lost in his daydreams about inventions that his parents and doctors ordered a test to check his hearing. In grade school, Musk was short, introverted, and bookish. He was bullied until he was fifteen.	He is now the founder, CEO, and chief engineer at SpaceX; an early-stage investor, CEO, and product architect of Tesla, Inc.; founder of The Boring Company and cofounder of Neuralink and OpenAI. A centibillionaire, Musk is one of the wealthiest people in the world.
P!NK (FEMALE POP SINGER)	Alecia Beth Moore (born September 8, 1979), known professionally as Pink (stylized as P!nk), is an American singer and songwriter. Although she went to Moore College of Art and Design, she dropped out after a year.	!Pink has sold over ninety million records worldwide, making her one of the world's best-selling music artists. Her career accolades include three Grammy Awards, two Brit Awards, a Daytime Emmy Award, and seven MTV Video Music Awards, including the Michael Jackson Video Vanguard Award. In 2009, Billboard named !Pink the Pop Songs Artist of the Decade. VH1 ranked her at number ten on its list of the 100 Greatest Women in Music.

THE ROCK (ACTOR)	Dwayne Johnson is the grand-son of professional wrestler Peter "High Chief" Fanene Maivia and the son of wrestler Rocky Johnson. With no plans to follow in his father's footsteps, Johnson played college football at the University of Miami until being slowed by injuries. With few prospects in professional football, Johnson turned to wrestling, debuting in the WWE.	He thrived in professional wrestling and is now one of the world's highest-grossing and highest-paid actors. In 2019, *Time Magazine* recognized him as one of the top 100 Most Influential People in the World.
DUDE PERFECT (SOCIAL MEDIA INFLUENCERS)	American sports and comedy group headquartered in Frisco, Texas. On April 9, 2009, a video of the group of friends perform-ing trick shots was released on YouTube. Within a week, the video received 200,000 views.	The channel is the current most-subscribed sports channel on YouTube and the sixteenth most-subscribed channel overall. They have an estimated net worth of over fifty million dollars.

KURT WARNER [SUPER BOWL MVP QUARTER- BACK IN NFL & PRO FOOTBALL HALL OF FAME MEMBER]	Played quarterback at the University of Northern Iowa and wasn't named the starting quarterback until his senior year. He didn't get drafted and spent four years without being named to an NFL roster. He played three seasons for the Iowa Barnstormers of the Arena Football League, played for the Amsterdam Admirals, and became the third-string quarterback for the St. Louis Rams in 1999.	Warner became the St. Louis Rams starting quarterback in 1999 and won the Super Bowl the same year. He played twelve seasons and started in three Super Bowls. Warner is now considered the NFL's greatest undrafted player of all time. He is the only undrafted player to be named NFL MVP and Super Bowl MVP and the only undrafted quarterback to lead his team to a Super Bowl victory. He is also the first quarterback to win the Super Bowl during his first season as the primary starter. Warner was inducted into the Pro Football Hall of Fame in 2017 and is the only player inducted into both the Pro Football Hall of Fame and Arena Football Hall of Fame.
GARTH BROOKS [COUNTRY MU- SIC LEGEND]	Played local clubs and traveled to Nashville in 1985 to get a record contract. Failed in this attempt and went back to playing local gigs.	In 2007, Brooks was named the best-selling solo artist in US history.

MICHAEL JORDAN (BASKETBALL LEGEND)	Attended Emsley A. Laney High School in Wilmington, North Carolina, where he tried out for the varsity basketball team during his sophomore year. At five feet eleven inches tall, he was deemed too short to play at that level and was cut from the team.	In 1999, ESPN named him the greatest North American athlete of the twentieth century. His individual accolades and accomplishments include five MVP awards, ten All-NBA First Team designations, nine All-Defensive First Team honors, fourteen NBA All-Star Game appearances, three All-Star MVP, ten scoring titles, three steals' titles, and six NBA Finals MVP awards.

Making conscious choices in pursuit of an *Extraordinary Life* means building up confidence and the decision-making muscle inside your mind. You can only build muscle through regular use. If you use that muscle regularly, you will strengthen it. If you don't, you will lose it and lose out on the choices that could have delivered a life filled with purpose and major accomplishments.

EPIPHANY AT THE PUBLIC POOL

In the summer of 2008, I had an experience—an *epiphany*—that would soon change my life forever! It was a hot day in Iowa, and I was at the public swimming pool with my son, Beau, who was four years old at the time. He was wearing a life jacket, swimming in the kiddie pool. I was in waist-deep water without my shirt on, and I weighed three hundred and ten pounds. It would be safe to say that I was scaring the women and confusing the babies because I was not in the best shape.

I dreamed of making some big changes physically, getting to a healthy weight, and living a healthy lifestyle, but I had always struggled with eating healthy. On this day, I was self-conscious about how I looked. While Beau and I played catch with a football in the water, I became bothered by the fact that he kept turning and watching the high school and college kids jumping off the diving boards. After watching the kids do front flips and backflips off the high and low boards, he turned, looked at me, and asked, "Dad, can I jump off that diving board?"

He didn't know how to swim, but because it was just he and I at the pool—his mom was not in attendance—after further consideration, I gave him the green light and we walked over to the diving board. He stood in line behind the long group of people while I waited by the lifeguard stand, prepared to jump in and save him like a Navy SEAL once he landed in the pool.

Beau finally got up to the diving board, but once he stepped up to walk down the plank, I could see he became nervous. He had made a choice to do something extraordinary but feared what that choice could mean. I encouraged him to keep walking and get to the edge. He followed my instruction and stood on the edge for quite some time, staring at the water. The line behind him just looked on, growing more and more impatient with each passing minute.

I encouraged Beau to jump by yelling "jump, jump, jump," but he did not budge. He kept shaking his head "no, no, no" while I kept saying "yes, yes, yes." Finally, I could see confidence in his eyes as he inched along to the end of the diving board. He tilted his body and leaned toward the water. As he fell in, I waited for him to bob back up to congratulate him. When he reached the surface, his smile was so big he could eat a banana sideways. He was so happy as he doggy paddled to the side of the pool and shouted, "Dad did you see my flip?"

It was fun to see him overcome fear to do something that, to him, was extraordinary. Of most importance was what he asked as soon as he got out of the pool: "Dad, can I do it again?" Anytime a person attempts something outside their fear barrier, and does not die but rather enjoys the process, they discover newfound confidence and competence to do it again. I agreed and positioned myself by the lifeguard stand once again as he waited in line.

When he got to the diving board, his attitude was completely different. There was a boldness about him. He stepped onto the diving board, looked over to me, and gave me a big thumbs up. Honestly, I became nervous, wondering what he was going to do next and how I would explain it to his mom!

Immediately after the thumbs up, he began running down the platform and jumped while throwing his legs over the top of his head and flipping off the diving board. After watching others do flips while he was in the kiddie pool, Beau could recreate their success at the age of four without any formal training. I was blown away by his decision and significant accomplishment. It was not because of his skill or technique but, rather, his choice to do something he wanted to do.

Growing up, I had always wanted to do a flip off a diving board but failed miserably. Being a bigger kid, I did not have the confidence and mindset necessary to pull it off. Many summers, I watched the other kids doing flips off diving boards, but when I tried to replicate their success, I floundered, resulting in a massive belly or back flop.

It was painful, not just physically but also mentally, when other people would laugh and make fun of me. I decided to stop trying to do the flip around age ten or twelve and became comfortable with being "the cannonball guy." It was not nearly as entertaining as the flip, but I could bring it and soak the lifeguard when needed.

When I saw Beau do his flip, it got me thinking that maybe I could do it as well. I saw what he had accomplished and how he did it, and I felt I could recreate the steps. As soon as he got out of the pool, I told him to go over by the lifeguard stand and that I was going to do a flip.

I waited in the long line on a hot day in a small town, overweight and without my shirt on. The longer I waited, the more I began to rethink my decision. When I finally got up to the diving board, I immediately felt the same fear that Beau had moments earlier.

Beau began motivating me now, saying "jump, jump, jump," and I was starting to shake my head just like he had, saying "no, no, no!" I finally felt the pressure of people waiting behind me and decided to test the diving board's capacity. I walked to the end of the board and bounced a little to see how springy it was.

I quickly discovered that diving boards had changed quite a bit in the last twenty-five years. I was used to diving off a firm plank with very little spring, but this board could increase or decrease the tension. When I bounced on it, I felt like the board went down, touched the water, and came back up, so I knew it had been adjusted to launch mode. With my size, I began to think that if I calculated my bounce incorrectly, I could end up in the next town!

I decided to just take off and do it. I got a big bounce, and then what had happened all those years ago came rushing back. I had not reached the rotation I needed, so I landed with a big back flop. The sting of the water slapping my back was painful enough, but even more painful was the fact that people were surrounding the pool watching me fail.

I came to the surface slowly and gazed into the eyes of the lifeguard, a young woman, and could see her holding her hand over her face laughing. Then came the shout-outs from friends in the community who witnessed this failure. "Good one, Bush," they bellowed. It brought back all the memories of how I had tried before and failed. But this time, I decided not to stop.

I made a fundamental shift that day. Once again, I went into *Cliff Climber* mode, and in my mind said I will not leave this pool today until I complete a flip. I could tell it was a different mindset, and I was committed to it. I was sick and tired of failing. I got back in line and tried again. Unfortunately, the second performance was not much better than the first. While Beau waited patiently, I got back in line and tried a third time. I learned from my mistakes and completed a front flip . . . off a low diving board . . . at three-hundred and ten pounds! It was a glorious feeling—a moment of triumph I relished for the first time in my life, all thanks to a daredevil four-year-old. Honestly, I felt like I had won the Olympics.

Beau and I became "the flip guys" that day, and it taught me a new lesson about never giving up and failing your way forward. Choosing to live an *Extraordinary Life* is all about embracing your fears and not allowing your past failures to prevent you from pursuing what matters to you most. In short, agreeing to make hard choices.

After completing the flip, Beau asked me if he could jump off the high dive. I said that was for adults. He told me that I was an adult and that I should jump off the high dive. I immediately regretted my response. I felt like I had just done something extraordinary but was not ready to do something extra-extraordinary! But this day was different so I said I would do it, and I was not going to just jump—I was going to flip!

As I climbed to the top of the high dive, my fear increased with every step. Once I got to the top, I could see rooftops of buildings and the tops of water towers! I realized why they called it the high dive because it is significantly higher than the other dive! I knew I could not spend much time thinking about it, so I just ran to the end, jumped, threw my legs over the top of my head and, miraculously, landed a flip on my first try.

That event awoke in me a new perspective on what was possible in my life. Agreeing to make hard choices to do something frightening and succeed got me thinking of all the other things I had been wanting to do but was too afraid to try.

I decided to get healthier later that year and enrolled in a personal health coaching program where I lost a hundred pounds. The mental barrier had been broken. I was a different person because of the choices I made to go above and beyond the usual, regular, and customary to do hard things. I was beginning to live an *Extraordinary Life* because I let go of fear, doubt, and uncertainty.

FLIP OR FEAR?

"DON'T DWELL ON WHAT WENT WRONG. INSTEAD, FOCUS ON WHAT TO DO NEXT. SPEND YOUR ENERGIES ON MOVING FORWARD TOWARD FINDING THE ANSWER."

– Dr. Denis Waitley

What is your flip? What have you been avoiding? Are you ready to make the fundamental choice to be, do, or have something extraordinary and overcome your fear of failure? Are you willing to let go of your past, limiting beliefs and self-doubt to pursue something that could be life-changing to you and to many others?

LIFE

Zig Ziglar once said the word "if" is exactly one half of the term "life." If you agree to make hard choices and live beyond fear, your life will be considerably different than if you do not. Will you be a *Cliff Climber, Cave Camper, Valley Dweller,* or *River Rafter?* The choice is yours.

Have you allowed fear to rule your life? I think we all have for way too long. It's time we embraced our fears and explored what lies beyond our comfort zone. Are you ready to make extraordinary choices that will empower you to live an *Extraordinary Life?*

"TOO MANY TOMORROWS AND ALL YOU'LL END UP WITH IS JUST A BUNCH OF EMPTY YESTERDAYS."

– Meredith Wilson, American composer, songwriter, and playwright

EXTRAORDINARY LIFE ACTION STEP: AGREE TO MAKE HARD CHOICES

"HAVE YOU BUILT YOUR CASTLES IN THE SKY? GOOD, THAT IS WHERE THEY SHOULD BE. NOW BUILD THE FOUNDATIONS UNDERNEATH THEM."

– Henry David Thoreau

It is good to have big dreams prioritized into a timeline, but that is not all you need to make them come true.

Just as we need architectural drawings when constructing a building or a road map when traveling to an unknown destination, we need a sound action plan if we hope to live our biggest dreams. Our dreams require action plans to help us break them down into smaller (and more achievable) goals, so we do not get overwhelmed with the magnitude of our dream.

Some people prefer to wander without a plan because they think developing one is hard and tedious. Actually, wandering aimlessly as a way of life is much harder in the long run! Without a solid action plan, we may never achieve anything we really want in life; we may end up wandering aimlessly, like countless dreamers who have lost their way.

If we lack an action plan, we may easily get lost, led astray, or become discouraged. We lack direction as to where we are, what the next step is, and how much farther the ultimate destination is from where we are now. Just like a road map or GPS navigation system gives us a clear sense of direction, a good action plan will alleviate all this uncertainty and provide the needed direction each day.

WHAT IS INSIDE AN ACTION PLAN?

A solid action plan consists of three items:

* A Purpose Statement
* S.M.A.R.T. Goals
* Action Steps

The **Purpose Statement** is the reason you want to realize your dream. What would realizing the dream do for you? Upon successfully achieving the dream, what benefits would you experience? By writing these REASONS down, you'll be reminded of them each time you review your action plan.

> ## "YOU'LL ACCOMPLISH YOUR DREAMS ONLY WHEN YOU HAVE ENOUGH REASONS TO ACCOMPLISH THEM BECAUSE WHEN THE WHY GETS STRONGER, THE HOW GETS EASIER."
> – Jim Rohn

S. M. A. R. T. Goals break your dream down into specific, measurable, achievable, realistic, and time-sensitive targets. Just thinking about your goals is not enough. You must act!

Action Steps are the specific activities you will undertake to support those SMART goals—activities you will want to review and refine regularly.

With all three elements in place, you will be able to chart your course and measure your performance in accomplishing the big dream. You will also have something concrete and achievable to focus your energy on each day. There's an old phrase: "How do you eat an elephant? One bite at a time." If you follow this philosophy, you will be on the right path.

"ONE HOUR OF PLANNING IS EQUAL TO EIGHT HOURS OF HARD LABOR."

– Benjamin Franklin

You have a choice: Plan now and work less, or plan later (or maybe not at all) and work more. Remember, the shortest distance between you and your dream is a straight line. The more complete your plan, the straighter the line. Once you create your plan, proceed to the next chapter to learn how to strengthen your commitment to carry it out and realize your dreams!

IMPORTANT QUESTIONS TO CONSIDER FOR YOUR PLAN

What goal would get me closer to this dream?

What do I need to do today or this week to better realize this dream?

What action will I take today?

"HE WHO EVERY MORNING PLANS THE TRANS-ACTION OF THE DAY AND FOLLOWS OUT THAT PLAN, CARRIES A THREAD THAT WILL GUIDE HIM THROUGH THE MAZE OF THE MOST BUSY LIFE. BUT WHERE NO PLAN IS LAID, WHERE THE DIS-POSAL OF TIME IS SURRENDERED MERELY TO THE CHANCE OF INCIDENCE, CHAOS WILL SOON REIGN."

- Victor Hugo, French poet, playwright, and human rights activist

USE THIS WORKSHEET TO CRAFT YOUR EXTRAORDINARY PHYSICAL WELLNESS PLAN

Download a copy of this planning tool at TheExtraordinaryLife.com.

Your Desired Outcome (Define your PEAK goal of what you want to accomplish, be, do, or have specifically in the area of physical wellness.):

_____

_____

Due Date:

Purpose (Why is this important?):

_____

_____

Goal #3

Action Step: _____ Due Date: _____

Action Step: _____ Due Date: _____

Goal #2

Action Step: _____ Due Date: _____

Action Step: _____ Due Date: _____

Goal #1

Action Step: _____ Due Date: _____

Action Step: _____ Due Date: _____

Your Current Reality (Define your current circumstances, challenges, pain, and problems.):

_____

USE THIS WORKSHEET TO CRAFT YOUR EXTRAORDINARY MENTAL WELLNESS PLAN

Download a copy of this planning tool at TheExtraordinaryLife.com.

Your Desired Outcome (Define your PEAK goal of what you want to accomplish, be, do, or have specifically in the area of physical wellness.):

_____

_____

Due Date:

Purpose (Why is this important?):

_____

_____

Goal #3

Action Step: _____ Due Date: _____

Action Step: _____ Due Date: _____

Goal #2

Action Step: _____ Due Date: _____

Action Step: _____ Due Date: _____

Goal #1

Action Step: _____ Due Date: _____

Action Step: _____ Due Date: _____

Your Current Reality (Define your current circumstances, challenges, pain, and problems.):

_____

USE THIS WORKSHEET TO CRAFT YOUR EXTRAORDINARY FINANCIAL WELLNESS PLAN

Download a copy of this planning tool at TheExtraordinaryLife.com.

Your Desired Outcome (Define your PEAK goal of what you want to accomplish, be, do, or have specifically in the area of physical wellness.):

_____

_____

Due Date:

Purpose (Why is this important?):

_____

_____

Goal #3

Action Step: _____ Due Date: _____

Action Step: _____ Due Date: _____

Goal #2

Action Step: _____ Due Date: _____

Action Step: _____ Due Date: _____

Goal #1

Action Step: _____ Due Date: _____

Action Step: _____ Due Date: _____

Your Current Reality (Define your current circumstances, challenges, pain, and problems.):

_____

CHAPTER 4

EXTRAORDINARY COMMITMENT #4
DECIDE TO FAIL FORWARD

"SUCCESS IS NOT A GLEAMING SHINY MOUNTAIN.
IT'S A PILE OF MISTAKES THAT YOU'RE STANDING
ON INSTEAD OF BURIED UNDER."

- Dave Ramsey, best-selling author and radio host

Commitment is what keeps you going when you encounter adversity and fail—which you will if you are pursuing an *Extraordinary Life*. Your decision to continue climbing *Extraordinary Life Mountain* when you've slid backward due to unfortunate circumstances, choices you've , or seemingly insurmountable barriers will dictate whether you live an *Extraordinary Life* or an ordinary one.

Many *Cliff Climbers* experience struggles and even failure in their effort to summit *Extraordinary Life Mountain.* They will see the *Cave Campers, Valley Dwellers,* and *River Rafters* succeeding to a certain level or experiencing less failure, pain, or challenges and wonder if hiking the mountain is really their calling. This is where we must use all our power to stay true to our calling, dreams, and mission.

Willpower can help a person get started on their journey, but we need more than willpower to fully realize our dreams because willpower has a limited reserve. It must be refilled with motivation and a strong purpose built on WHY you want to achieve your dream. Disgust, frustration, and other emotional conflicts with your current circumstances can get you moving, but you need a combination of *willpower, skill-power* and *thrill-power,* to achieve your biggest dreams and aspirations.

Skill-power is an unlimited resource that many top *Cliff Climbers* have tapped into to realize their dreams. They have discovered the more skills you learn, the more you can become, and the more you become, the more you can achieve. When you see this process working for you, it becomes a habit. Becoming self-motivated, developing the skills to control your mind, and staying focused on achieving your dream is critical for success.

Thrill-power is also an unlimited resource you can tap into. This is where you find joy in doing the work necessary in the process of realizing your dreams. Surrounding yourself with people who have fun doing the work, choosing to laugh at your mistakes and rejoice in your progress, is an excellent recipe for lifelong success.

THE LINCOLN FACTOR

Abraham Lincoln is my favorite example of someone who embodied the principle of commitment. Lincoln's life stands as a monument to single-minded purpose. He rose from a very humble station and endured fiercer hardships during his span on this earth than most of us can imagine. Yet, he ended up making an extraordinary contribution to this nation, shepherding it through a bitter civil war and securing the Union. If you ever need an example of the role undying commitment can play in overcoming obstacles, consider the milestones of Lincoln's life.

1816: Lincoln's frontier family moves from Kentucky to Indiana in response to a dispute over who has title to the Lincoln family farm. Seven-year-old Abraham, large for his age, has worked long hours to help ensure the family's success in Kentucky; he continues to work long hours in Indiana.

1818: Lincoln's mother dies. He is nine years old at the time.

1831: Lincoln loses his job as a clerk when the merchant who employs him goes out of business.

1832: Lincoln runs for the Illinois State Legislature. He loses.

1833: Lincoln borrows money to start a business; it goes under, and he is unable to pay the debts. His possessions are seized by the sheriff.

1834: Unable to afford law school, Lincoln begins teaching himself law.

1834: Lincoln runs for the state legislature again and wins.

1835: The early love of Lincoln's life, Ann Rutledge, dies. He enters a profound depression.

1838 — 1839: Lincoln makes two attempts to become the speaker of the Illinois House of Representatives, failing each time.

1842: Lincoln marries Mary Todd, a deeply eccentric woman who would, years after Lincoln's death, eventually be committed to a mental asylum. The couple has four sons, but only one, Robert, would survive into adulthood.

1843: Lincoln seeks the Whig party's nomination for Congress and loses.

1848: Following instructions from his party, Lincoln does not run for reelection to Congress.

1849: Lincoln is passed over for the plum patronage position of Commissioner of the General Land Office, a federal post he sought after stepping down from Congress.

1854: Lincoln seeks his party's nomination for the US Senate and loses.

1856: Lincoln's name is placed in nomination for the vice presidency and loses.

1858: Lincoln finally secures his party's nomination for a US Senate seat and loses.

1860: Lincoln is elected President of the United States.

Commitment is what transforms a promise into reality. It is making the time when there is none. Coming through time after time after time, year after year after year. Commitment is the stuff character is made of; the power to change the face of things.

Any of Lincoln's setbacks would have been enough to bring down a lesser person. What made the difference for Lincoln? Commitment—that which "transforms a promise into reality." Are you prepared to summon the same kind of extraordinary commitment to your mission in life that Lincoln summoned? Are you ready to bounce back when adversity strikes? Remember, *Extraordinary Life Cliff Climbers* become extraordinary because of their commitment and persistence regardless of the circumstances!

Many people who say they want to live an *Extraordinary Life* fail to do so because they are short on persistence and commitment. When the first (second, third, or fourth) obstacle comes along, they give up. What they do not realize is these obstacles— the apparent lack of resources, the skeptical or dismissive voices of other people, the sudden changes in the larger economy or any other challenge you care to name—are not stop signs, they are indications of human character.

I call the act of responding to obstacles with more commitment, as opposed to less, "The Lincoln Factor." All *Cliff Climbers* make it part of their personal character to expand commitment in the face of opposition.

"THE ULTIMATE MEASURE OF A MAN IS NOT WHERE HE STANDS IN MOMENTS OF COMFORT AND CONVENIENCE, BUT WHERE HE STANDS AT TIMES OF CHALLENGE AND CONTROVERSY."

– Dr. Martin Luther King, Jr.

The central reality of human experience is "failure." The real question is not whether we will fail but how we will respond when it happens. Notice that I placed quotation marks around the word because apparent failure is nothing more than a test of our personal commitment to persist. It is better to think of this as "the failure test" than as some divine sign we should not pursue our goals after all. Some of us will pass the failure test—others will not.

Here is a brief list of just a few of the extraordinary people who made The Lincoln Factor a driving reality in their lives and passed the failure test with flying colors:

- By the time J.K. Rowling had finished the first of the *Harry Potter* books, she was divorced, on welfare, and with a child to support. All twelve major publishers rejected the *Harry Potter* manuscript.
- The Beatles failed an audition with Decca Records, whose talent scout dismissed their sound and warned their manager that guitar groups were "on the way out."
- Albert Einstein dropped out of high school and failed his entrance exam for college.
- Walt Disney was fired from a newspaper job because he lacked "imagination" and had "no original ideas."

The only people who never fail are those who never try anything new! For the rest of us, the question is . . . what happens AFTER "failure"?

One secret to staying committed to your dream(s) is to spend considerable time thinking about it with a positive expectation.

A particularly effective way to do this is to create a vision board—something you can see every day that incorporates vivid pictures of all the benefits you will receive from pursuing your dream. Also, create a long, written list of reasons to act on your life mission and review those regularly.

You must create commitment daily and act daily if you wish to turn your dream into reality. You need to do something every day to support your goal, regardless of how big or little what you are doing appears to be. If your goal is to write the next *New York Times* best seller, write a little bit of it each day no matter what! Your motive will strengthen your actions in support of your goal, and your actions will, in turn, improve your motivation.

Your ability to stay committed to your dreams requires daily motivation, the act of having an idea or motive consistently driving you to act!

Motive + Action = Motivation

WATCHING A DREAM CRASH AND BURN

After playing football, I began a career in the mortgage industry, deciding to become successful in the business world. I started as a mortgage loan officer and was quickly promoted to management. Eventually, I became one of the co-owners of a mortgage company with seventeen offices in three states. I leveraged the experiences from pursuing my dream of playing professional football into my new career and saw how it accelerated my progress in achieving extraordinary business results.

In 2004, I began to feel a strong calling to follow my childhood dream of becoming a peak performance coach and motivational speaker. I wanted to inspire others daily to realize their dreams and change their world. I had reached a high level of success in the mortgage industry and coached others in the mortgage, real estate, insurance, and financial services world. I was seeing great results, so I felt ready to pursue my next dream.

I invested my life savings into building a web-based peak performance coaching software program, believing it would significantly propel my speaking and coaching career. I received lots of great feedback from key influencers and decided to leave my steady, executive-level income in the mortgage industry to jump into living my dream as a peak performance coach and speaker.

I launched my coaching business with lots of fanfare and visions of success. It was like a rocket ship taking off. I was flying high doing speaking events and coaching top industry leaders. Then, in 2008, it crashed midair when the mortgage industry crisis hit.

Hundreds of companies that would hire me as a professional speaker went out of business. Many top entrepreneurs and sales executives who hired me as a peak performance coach lost 25 –50 percent of their income due to the downturn in the financial markets. Some started defaulting on their coaching payments and asked to cancel their coaching contracts.

That period was extremely painful, to put it mildly. I went from "cliff climbing" to sliding down the mountain and falling down the *Waterfall of Life* in a matter of months. I began self-medicating with unhealthy habits and choices. The pain would abate for a short while, but my harmful habits continued to make life worse. I felt like a failure as a husband, dad, entrepreneur, and leader. I kept looking into my past and wondering why I decided to walk away from such a high income to risk it all pursuing this dream. I was depressed, discouraged, and highly disappointed.

I had some difficult decisions to make if I was ever going to turn it around, but I was determined to commit to NEVER QUIT!

MAKE A COMMITMENT TO "NEVER QUIT"

Life does not always go according to plan; sometimes, we veer off course. When that happens, we need to have a motto or message we can repeat out loud that helps us get back on track.

My favorite example of a motivating message comes from the US military. As you may know, the Navy SEALS are legendary for their commitment to their mission, sometimes in the face of hardships that most of us cannot imagine.

A former Navy SEALS trainer was once speaking in front of a large audience on commitment. When he concluded his remarks, he asked the listeners whether they had any questions. A member of the audience stood up and said, "Yes, I have a question. What happens in the SEAL training that prepares your people to endure such dire circumstances in battle or while in captivity?"

The trainer responded, "We teach them to NEVER QUIT."

The questioner would not accept the answer. "Come on!" he persisted. "You must use some sort of special program to train them to endure things like emotional abuse, isolation, deprivation, torture, and life-threatening injuries without ever losing their commitment to the mission."

The Navy SEALS trainer responded quite firmly, "We train them to NEVER QUIT."

The reason why the Navy SEALS are so highly regarded in their field is that they NEVER QUIT. They are legendary for their self-discipline, and the endlessly-repeated motivating message, NEVER QUIT, is the reason why.

Now let me ask you a question: What if you decided to NEVER QUIT on your plans, dreams, and goals, and make that message part of your personal identity? Where could you go in the world if you made a personal commitment to make NEVER QUIT your motivating message whenever you hit an obstacle? Where would you be in your life one year from now if you made a habit of repeating that message to yourself, out loud, at least one hundred times each day?

Make NEVER QUIT your motivating message—the message you repeat to yourself whenever you veer off course.

I used this message to rebound from my failures and challenges and because I did, I have discovered new peaks and altitudes of success far beyond where I had been before I experienced failure.

CREATING A LEGACY

My most harrowing experience with the Lincoln Factor was in 2010. One day, I was presenting a day-long seminar on building a successful business and achieving healthy finances. Approximately halfway through the presentation, I checked my phone. I had several missed calls from my wife, so I knew immediately something was wrong.

I called my wife and she said that all the money in our bank accounts was gone! I had leveraged myself with credit card debt to become successful in business but, in doing so, fell behind and did not pay my taxes on time. I set up a payment plan to repay the taxes but, unfortunately, I didn't stay current, so the IRS decided to empty my bank accounts to pay off the debt.

I was always successful in my career and never asked anyone for financial help. I took a lot of pride in providing for my family and became completely discouraged and disappointed when this happened. It was probably the lowest point in my life.

Yet here I was, leading a seminar, educating people on living their dreams, coaching them on business and financial success principles, when those very same principles did not create the success I hoped for. I felt like a fraud. It was the ultimate test in commitment, and I had a choice to make. I chose to stay committed to the seminar attendees and shared passionately, with enthusiasm and dedication, the principles I believed in.

Persistence is a key ingredient in any extraordinary accomplishment. I never recall hearing a success story of someone accomplishing something extraordinary where there wasn't a point in time when they thought it wasn't going to happen. I can personally say that every significant accomplishment in my life has required persistence and commitment, including . . .

- Earning my Bachelor of Arts degree
- Losing one hundred pounds
- Running a half-marathon
- Being married to the love of my life
- Raising our three children
- Overcoming failure and achieving success in my career
- Building successful businesses
- Developing a successful team

These principles come with risks of failure, but they also come with enormous opportunities to succeed. There are no guarantees of success in life, of course. Your *Extraordinary Life* might look extraordinarily different than you planned or dreamt. But if you commit today to go above and beyond what is usual, regular, and customary and never quit pursuing your dreams, I promise you will not be disappointed in what you accomplish. You will achieve extraordinary things and become an *Extraordinary Life Cliff Climber*. Why? Because those who stay committed to the passions in their heart, and the dreams in their mind, will always become more, learn more, and achieve more!

In 2010, I persisted and kept believing in the principles of success and coaching others on them. Because of my persistence I was able to overcome the financial challenges and poor decision-making. I chose to NEVER QUIT, and our lives have been blessed because of hard work, effort, and consistency in doing hard things even when it felt like it wouldn't work. You can experience the same if you choose to fail forward.

EXTRAORDINARY LIFE ACTION STEP: DECIDE TO FAIL FORWARD

Implementing our plans and acting on our dreams usually comes down to three things:

- getting motivated and inspired enough to take the initiative;
- effectively managing our priorities;
- failing forward while maintaining motivation and inspiration.

How do you motivate yourself to tackle your biggest dreams even when you fail?

Do you have a plan in place to stay motivated?

You should! The best way is to be active in accomplishing tasks that move you closer to your dream. You can also stay motivated by renewing your mind with positive, inspirational resources, such as books, podcasts, videos, Bible verses, inspirational quotes, and similar materials.

There are days when staying motivated is hard for even the best *Extraordinary Life Cliff Climber*. Most of us require the assistance and support of others. There are times when we do not feel like tackling a new dream (or staying persistent with an old one that has not come true yet). Motivation comes and goes. In fact, motivation comes quickly and leaves even more unexpectedly than it arrived! We hear a song that motivates us to do something special and an hour later, we forget what it was that moved us. We attend a seminar and get energized entirely to make a change in our life, taking copious notes on all the changes we are going to make. The next day, we can't even find our notes!

We are so bombarded with forces competing for our attention—advertisements, phone calls, kids, work, and so on—that, often, the urgent outweighs the essential and something I call the "Law of Declining Intent" takes over.

The Law of Declining Intent says if you fail to act on an idea the moment you are motivated to, the odds of you ever acting on it begin to decline rapidly from that point forward.

PLAN YOUR PRIORITIES

We are all given twenty-four precious hours per day, no more and no less. We must become crystal clear about the priorities we set for those hours. Let us act on our highest priorities first and leave all minor priorities to whatever time is left over. Only then will our time management efforts be successful. If we approach things haphazardly or ignore high-priority items in favor of low-priority ones, we will not get much traction on our goals.

Begin managing your priorities by scheduling the highest into your daily calendar. Use the table on the following page to assist you in planning your *Extraordinary Life*. Use the words that start with the letter "F" to guide you to schedule appointments with yourself so you can invest the needed time for your faith, fitness, family, friendships, fun, finances, and the most important tasks in your firm or career. Be vigilant with the appointments you schedule with yourself. When you hit a bump in the road—which you will—keep your priorities in place, no matter how dire the emergency seems. Find a way to prioritize the solution . . . then schedule a time to act on it!

"WE WOULD ACCOMPLISH MANY MORE THINGS IF WE DID NOT THINK OF THEM AS IMPOSSIBLE."

- Vince Lombardi, two-time NFL Super Bowl champion coach of the Green Bay Packers

TIME	MON.	TUE.	WED.	THU.	FRI.	SAT.	SUN.
5:00AM							
5:30AM							
6:00AM							
6:30AM							
7:00AM							
7:30AM							
8:00AM							
8:30AM							
9:00AM							
9:30AM							
10:00AM							
10:30AM							
11:00AM							
11:30AM							
12:00PM							
12:30PM							
1:00PM							
1:30PM							
2:00PM							
2:30PM							
3:00PM							
3:30PM							
4:00PM							
4:30PM							
5:00PM							
5:30PM							
6:00PM							
6:30PM							
7:00PM							
7:30PM							
8:00PM							
8:30PM							
9:00PM							
9:30PM							
10:00PM							

FAITH   FAMILY   FINANCES   FIRM/WORK   FITNESS   FRIENDS   FUN

BREAK THROUGH THE OBSTACLES AND DECIDE TO FAIL FORWARD!

"EVERY DAY, YOU MAY MAKE PROGRESS. EVERY STEP MAY BE FRUITFUL. YET, THERE WILL STRETCH OUT BEFORE YOU AN EVER-LENGTHENING, EVER-ASCENDING, EVER-IMPROVING PATH. YOU KNOW YOU WILL NEVER GET TO THE END OF THE JOURNEY. BUT THIS, SO FAR FROM DISCOURAGING, ONLY ADDS TO THE JOY AND GLORY OF THE CLIMB."

- Winston Churchill

Obstacles are a fact of life, yet every successful person learns to break through them. Here are six breakthrough strategies you can use when challenges present themselves en route to your goal.

1. **Review your vision board.** Today's struggles can distract us from the hope of tomorrow. However, reviewing a vision board with photos and images of our dreams helps us rethink what is possible.

2. **Adjust your philosophy and perspective as needed.** Sometimes, we just need to make a tiny change in our philosophy, our way of looking at the world, to get past a roadblock. Did you "fail" at something in the past or learn how something does not or did not work? Our perspective determines our mindset. Our mindset dictates how we show up in the world. When we change the way we see the world, it begins to change. Your MESS can lead to a powerful MESSage, and the bigger the TEST, the greater your TESTimony of success will become!

3. **Review your plan often.** A good *Cliff Climber* makes constant adjustments based on the conditions they encounter but never strays far from the plan. The same goes for those who wish to find a life of success and significance. We must keep reviewing our plan(s) and maintaining our course so we don't veer off course. Review your action plan at least once a month! Pay particular attention to the third part of the Action Steps plan to support your goal. What is getting you closer to your goal? What is not? What needs to be reconsidered?

4. **Hold yourself accountable.** Do not accept excuses, especially when you are offering them to yourself. Excuses will only prevent you from living your dreams. You, and you alone, are responsible for executing your action plan. Do not waste time and energy blaming others!

5. **Seek out positive associations.** Make a promise to yourself about how you plan to act, then share it with your spouse, significant other, or trusted friend. You will be more motivated to execute your plan!

   Positive people go where positive people go. This is a simple rule that most people fail to leverage! You must find a few positive people you can associate with and share your dreams with regularly. Birds of a feather really do flock together, so invest your time with the right flock! To paraphrase some ancient wisdom: Seek the right people and you shall find them, knock and the door will be opened, ask and you shall receive! Start assembling your success team today!

6. **Create and sustain a positive belief system.** Everything—absolutely everything—that happens to you happens for a reason, either as an opportunity or a lesson. Start thinking like this day in and day out . . . and you will start to think like a leader. That is a prerequisite for breaking through obstacles!

7. **Act immediately on whatever it is you feel inspired to do.** Begin developing your action plan for the weight you want

to lose, the business you want to start, or the trip you want to take—and do it now! Action is an internal motivator that inspires you to take more action.

8. **Invest in yourself and purchase resources you can use consistently to regain motivation whenever it lapses.** These may be books, movies, audio and video programs, podcasts, blogs, or music that changes your emotional state. Good books are essential! *Extraordinary Life Cliff Climbers* are extraordinary readers; they know if they grow mentally, they will grow personally and professionally as well.

Let us define what you are committed to and where you will invest time to realize your dreams. In the next chapter, I will give you a challenge to accelerate your progress and help you overcome the barriers to achieve your goals faster than you ever thought possible.

"ALL PERSONAL BREAKTHROUGHS BEGIN WITH A CHANGE IN BELIEFS."

- Anthony Robbins, best-selling author, coach, speaker, and philanthropist

IMPORTANT QUESTIONS TO CONSIDER:

What are you deeply committed to accomplishing?

How will you strengthen your commitment?

What have been your biggest barriers to staying committed in the past, and how will you overcome them in the future?

How can your past failures help you succeed in the future?

What are the consequences if you do not follow through on your commitments?

CHAPTER 5

EXTRAORDINARY COMMITMENT #5
EXPAND YOUR PERSPECTIVE

WHAT GETS US INTO TROUBLE IS NOT WHAT WE DON'T KNOW. IT'S WHAT WE KNOW FOR SURE THAT JUST AIN'T SO.

- Mark Twain, American writer, humorist, entrepreneur, publisher, and lecturer

Harold Abrahams, a British Olympic runner, hired a man named Sam Mussabini as his personal performance coach. Mr. Mussabini asked Harold to run around the track. When he was done, Mussabini explained to Abrahams that he could coach him to run the race "two extra steps" faster—and those two extra steps, could win him the gold medal in the Olympics.

Abrahams made Mussabini his coach, got the two extra steps and won the gold medal in 1924. The story is retold in the Oscar-winning movie *Chariots of Fire*. It shows us how a professional coach's perspective and insight can help someone become better than they could on their own.

Extraordinary athletes have coaches to help them get extraordinary results. Leaders who want to go beyond what is usual, regular, and customary in their lives also need coaches who can take them farther than they can take themselves.

Why is having a coach so important?

We know what we know. We don't know what we don't know. A coach brings some critical pieces to the success puzzle you will not find anywhere else:

- Strategic perspective, insights, and knowledge different from your own, along with the ability to identify "blind spots" you cannot see.
- Resources, tools, and tactics to help one accomplish the mission in less time with less effort and fewer mistakes.
- Accountability, motivation, and encouragement to help us go beyond what is comfortable.

Once someone has reached the peak of success with the help of a coach, you will find that person rarely takes on a major project, dream, or mission without one ever again.

"ACCOUNTABILITY BREEDS RESPONSE-ABILITY."

- Stephen Covey, best-selling author of the book *The 7 Habits of Highly Effective People*

THE COACH

The word *coach* comes from a town called Kocs in Hungary. Back in 1556, the residents of Kocs began to make large carriages that would take people from wherever they were to where they wanted to go. This large carriage was the beginning of what we know as the stagecoach.

A personal coach is like a stagecoach. The primary aim of the coach is to help the leader get from where they are to wherever they want to be. Helping the leader make this trip successfully is the only agenda of the coach, and the leader's success depends on the coach's ability to close this gap.

Without a coach in one's life, leaders can experience:

- Lack of Accountability
- Lack of Focus
- Lack of Direction
- Lack of Perspective
- Lack of Systems
- Lack of Balance

These symptoms can often lead to an ordinary life that produces ordinary results. A leader who settles for dwelling in the *Valley of Complacency* after accomplishing a certain level of success will never go beyond yesterday's achievements.

A coach can help challenge a leader to break out of this rut by bringing their dream(s) back into view, keeping them in focus. Leaders are constantly challenged by the elements around them, and it becomes tiring to continue climbing their *Extraordinary Life* mountain. Extraordinary coaches understand this and know where to go to help the leader find the courage to continue the journey to excellence.

Often, we think of a coach as someone who works face-to-face to inspire an individual or team to win a championship. This is just one example. Coaching can come in a variety of forms, including:

- A personal or professional growth book, video, podcast, or audio program
- Interactive websites, blogs, or other virtual resources
- Live training courses or workshops
- A mentor or accountability partner
- A mastermind group of individuals who challenge and coach one another
- A personal coach who works with you one-on-one

To live an *Extraordinary Life*, we all need some form of coaching to go beyond what is usual, regular, and customary in our lives. Coaches give us the EXTRA edge we need to make our lives *exceptional to a marked extent*. Resolve to find a coach or the coaching resources that will take you to the next level!

WHERE YOU ARE TODAY >>> COACHING >>> YOUR DREAMS

I have had many athletic and sports performance coaches who pushed me to achieve physical accomplishments. I have also had health, life, business, and spiritual coaches and mentors who have done the same in other areas of my life. The experience is quite extraordinary for those who are mentally ready to embrace the coaching and be accountable to their dreams and goals.

An extraordinary coach is not someone who tells you what to do but, rather, someone you develop a trusting relationship with who awakens you to your true potential by asking important questions to tap into your motivation. They empower you to develop a growth mindset versus maintaining a fixed mindset to discover the greatness that lies within you. They guide you to resources to assist you in becoming more educated, competent, and confident in your ability. They provide a system for success and encourage you to break through the barriers to extraordinary results by reminding you what is possible for those who do the work.

My personal health coaches did not just tell me what to eat. They taught me to think differently about the value of my health, the impact of my surroundings on my daily choices, and the importance of consuming quality foods. They showed me different ways to exercise and its benefits, the hidden benefits of sleep, strategies to manage stress, and the power of association, and how it impacted my health choices and decisions.

My life and leadership coaches revealed to me the value of significance over success, how to prioritize my life, how to become intrinsically and extrinsically motivated to overcome barriers I faced, and how to develop an extraordinary mindset to go above and beyond what is usual, regular, and customary to achieve exceptional results to a very marked extent.

My career, financial, and business coaches exposed me to opportunities for vocational growth. They taught me how to deliver more value to the marketplace to grow my income, influence, success, and significance to achieve my career, financial, and business dreams and goals.

Do you have coaches in your life who are assisting you to expand your perspective? Are you investing in your personal and professional growth and development? Remember, the experiences of others compress time. You can either pay by gaining experience on your own over time or pay someone else to share their learning experiences with you. My experience is that you will earn back your outlay quickly if you invest in quality coaching.

In the next chapter, we'll discuss how you can measure your progress and determine your return on your time, money, and energy investment.

EXTRAORDINARY LIFE ACTION STEP:
EXPAND YOUR PERSPECTIVE

Do you consider yourself coachable, open-minded, and someone who has a growth mindset and is willing to learn new ways of looking at opportunities, obstacles, and challenges?

Who have you been personally coached, mentored, or trained by In the past?

Where do you feel you could benefit the most from expanding your perspective and/or coaching right now (or in the future)? (Check all the boxes below that apply)

☐ Accountability   ☐ Assistance with clarifying/prioritizing goals

☐ Mentorship   ☐ Focus

☐ Planning   ☐ Strategies to achieve your goals

☐ Motivation   ☐ Encouragement/Guidance/Optimism

☐ Other: _____

How much focused time are you spending each day/week on personal and professional growth activities? (i.e., reading, watching videos/webinars, listening to audio programs, and/or attending events?)

In what area of your life do you feel you have the greatest opportunity for improvement to live a more *Extraordinary Life?*

What are the questions you need to be asked to keep you more accountable to your realizing your dreams and accomplishing your goals?

What will you commit to reading, watching, attending, and/or listening to regularly to grow your motivation, mindset, skills, and activity level in the next one to twelve months?

Who are the people (mentor, accountability buddy, coach, or other person) you will share your goals and/or challenges with and who will encourage you and hold you accountable? (List their names below)

CHAPTER 6

EXTRAORDINARY COMMITMENT #6
RESOLVE TO ACHIEVE
YOUR GOALS

"LEARN FROM THE PAST, BUT DON'T LIVE THERE.
BUILD ON WHAT YOU KNOW SO THAT YOU DON'T
REPEAT MISTAKES. RESOLVE TO LEARN SOMETHING
NEW EVERY DAY. BECAUSE EVERY TWENTY-FOUR
HOURS, YOU HAVE THE OPPORTUNITY TO HAVE THE
BEST DAY OF YOUR LIFE."

- Harvey McKay, seven-time, *New York TImes* best-selling
author of *Swim with the Sharks Without Being Eaten Alive*

Leaders who want to live an *Extraordinary Life* must approach life much the same way a top-performing athlete does when desiring to be the best at their game. Athletes who are serious about becoming extraordinary at what they do resolve to do whatever it takes to make it happen.

This requires time and effort in planning, practice, preparation, failing, coaching, personal/professional growth, and persistence. You will have to do the same. Only, in your case, the big event is not a single competition, season, or career, it's the rest of your life.

My vision is for you to accept the challenge and complete all the necessary activities to design and live your own *Extraordinary Life* and resolve to realize your dreams and change your world. It will be so worth it!

The definition of the word *resolve* is to decide firmly on a course of action and to declare or decide by a formal resolution and vote.

Are you ready to make a decision to live an *Extraordinary Life* and achieve your goals?

There's nothing that can stop a made-up mind and a person who resolves to do something extraordinary. When you decide you are sick and tired of being sick and tired, and you finally agree to do hard things, your world is forever changed.

"NEVER AGAIN CLUTTER YOUR DAYS OR NIGHTS WITH SO MANY MENIAL AND UNIMPORTANT THINGS THAT YOU HAVE NO TIME TO ACCEPT A REAL CHALLENGE WHEN IT COMES ALONG. THIS APPLIES TO PLAY AS WELL AS WORK. A DAY MERELY SURVIVED IS NO CAUSE FOR CELEBRATION. YOU ARE NOT HERE TO FRITTER AWAY YOUR PRECIOUS HOURS WHEN YOU HAVE THE ABILITY TO ACCOMPLISH SO MUCH BY MAKING A SLIGHT CHANGE IN YOUR ROUTINE. NO MORE BUSY WORK. NO MORE HIDING FROM SUCCESS. LEAVE TIME, LEAVE SPACE, TO GROW. NOW! NOT TOMORROW!"

- Og Mandino, legendary author and speaker

EXTRAORDINARY LIFE ACTION STEP: RESOLVE TO ACHIEVE YOUR GOALS

A proven model for success:

- The more you learn . . . the more you can become...
- The more you become . . . the more you can *measurably* achieve . . .
- The more you achieve . . . the more you can learn . . .
- The more you learn . . . the more you can become . . . (This model repeats continuously!)

This book has given you a lot to learn about living an *Extraordinary Life*. Now it's time to become more and achieve more to live your *Extraordinary Life*. Resolve to complete the action steps and pursue your calling, dreams, and goals with relentless commitment and measure your progress!

"THE UNEXAMINED LIFE IS NOT WORTH LIVING."
– Socrates

By taking time to reflect on your plan, progress, and accomplishments, you will learn more about what you are truly capable of achieving with the time, talents, skills, and abilities you have been given. Do not let another month, week, or day go by without measuring your progress. By determining what you are achieving, you will maintain focus, balance, and direction in your life.

"WHAT GETS MEASURED GETS DONE."
- Peter Drucker, leadership expert

Just as a mountain climber reviews their map frequently to make sure they are on the right path, so you must take time to review what you are achieving in your life. Find out what is working so you can ramp that up! If you are not making progress toward accomplishing your action plan, find out why and do whatever it takes to resolve the problem sooner rather than later.

Measuring the outcomes they generate is where many people start losing steam on their journey to success. That is a shame because knowing what you are measuring and how often you want to measure it is a great way to motivate yourself!

Here's What We Want to Measure

- Our dreams – Are they clearly defined? Are they really ours or someone else's?
- Our action plans – Do we have a clear plan of action with attainable goals and specific action steps to take?
- Our progress – Are we seeing measurable progress on the plans we've established? Are we headed in the right direction?
- Our use of time – Are we squandering valuable time on activities unrelated to our goals and dreams?

Here's How Often We Should Measure

- End of the day – Did we do what we needed to do?
- End of the week – Was our week productive?
- End of the month – Were our monthly goals accomplished?
- End of the quarter – Are there achievements to celebrate?
- End of the year – Was the past year successful? How do we know? And by the way, what is the reward?

By measuring our growth and development, we can reenergize, revitalize, and refocus ourselves on what matters most right now.

Schedule the dates you plan to review and measure your progress now and set a recurring reminder in your calendar. Come back to this book and check off each of the months you review your plan, and you will be on your way to your *Extraordinary Life*!

January	February	March
☐ April	☐ May	☐ June
☐ July	☐ August	☐ September
☐ October	☐ November	☐ December
☐	☐	☐

Consider Using These Tools to Measure Your Progress

- Personal Assessments – Use the *Extraordinary Life* assessment (physical/mental/financial) included in this book.
- Journaling – Use a journal to write down your thoughts and actions, to plan out your day in the morning, or to recap your progress in the evening.
- Time Tracking – Track every activity you do for one week. See where you are really spending your time.
- Peer Feedback – Ask your peers, coworkers, or spouse or significant other for feedback on your growth and development.
- Coaching – Hire a personal coach to help you track your progress over a period and use the free online coaching resources at TheExtraordinaryLife.com.

"WHAT YOU MEASURE IS WHAT YOU GET. WHAT YOU REWARD IS WHAT YOU GET. BY NOT ALIGNING MEASUREMENTS AND REWARDS, YOU OFTEN GET WHAT YOU'RE NOT LOOKING FOR."

- Jack Welch, Former CEO of GE

SUMMARY

**Will you make Extraordinary Commitment #1
and *Live Your Calling*?**

The ringing sound you keep hearing regarding the accomplishment of your dreams will not stop. We need more *Extraordinary Life Cliff Climbers* like you so we can benefit from your achievements.

**Will you make Extraordinary Commitment #2
and *Engage in Your Dreams*?**

It will take time to discover the dream(s) that act(s) as the catalyst in your life. Finding this agent that accelerates positive change is going to take some trial and error. You must sift through the different thoughts, dreams, and ideas and find those you know you have been called to act upon. It is your ultimate purpose in life to fulfill the dreams you have been given.

Will you make Extraordinary Commitment #3 and *Agree to Make Hard Choices?*

Every day that passes brings you one day closer to the end of your life. It is the nature of time to run out, and you will find as you age, time will move even faster than it does now. There is no time like today to start living an *Extraordinary Life.* Will you choose to live as if each day were a precious jewel, destined to vanish forever in just twenty-four hours? The choice is up to you!

Will you make Extraordinary Commitment #4 and *Decide to Fail Forward?*

You will undoubtedly face many obstacles on your journey. But will you keep pressing on regardless of the challenges you encounter? Will you make The Commitment required of all practical dreamers? Will you make the Lincoln Factor part of your own *Extraordinary Life?* Will you stay the course and follow your dreams?

Will you make Extraordinary Commitment #5 and *Expand Your Perspective?*

The most accomplished leaders know they cannot do it alone. They get ideas and support from the absolute best experts and coaches. So become a serious *Cliff Climber* and follow their example. Be both humble and assertive in pursuing your goal. When you are ready to be coached, the coach will appear.

Will you make Extraordinary Commitment #6 and *Resolve to Achieve Your Goals?*

The Challenge will be the most difficult part of your journey. It is where the heavy lifting and hard work is done . . . but it is also where *Extraordinary Life Cliff Climbers* are born and developed.

Be extraordinary and take this critical step! Most ordinary people will skip this step and make excuses for why they do not need it or simply procrastinate the opportunity away.

If your answer is "Yes" to the questions above, you will undoubtedly become a *Cliff Climber*, conquer yourself, and summit your very own *Extraordinary Life Mountain!*

See www.TheExtraordinaryLife.com for FREE online resources to help you complete the steps, embrace the Six Extraordinary Commitments, and **COMPLETE THE *EXTRAORDINARY LIFE* CHALLENGE!**

HOW YOU RESPOND TO THE CHALLENGE IN THE SECOND HALF WILL DETERMINE WHAT YOU BECOME AFTER THE GAME—WHETHER YOU ARE A WINNER OR A LOSER.

- Lou Holtz, author, motivational speaker, and former NCAA Football Coach of the Year

LIVE AN EXTRAORDINARY LIFE!

90 DAY *EXTRAORDINARY LIFE* CHALLENGE

(see complete details at www.TheExtraordinaryLife.com)

- [ ] Read the book and complete the action steps after each chapter
- [ ] Follow us on social media and join our *Extraordinary Life* Facebook Group
- [ ] Download and utilize the *Extraordinary Life* Daily Planner for 90 days
- [ ] Complete the *Extraordinary Life* Online Course
- [ ] Refer someone else to complete the challenge
- [ ] Share your success and progress with us after 90 days

Those who complete the challenge checklist receive a special, exclusive gift from us for living an *Extraordinary Life*!

ACKNOWLEDGMENTS

To my wife Kristen and our three children Cassidy, Morgan, and Beau, I want to say thank you for the major roles you all play in helping me live an *Extraordinary Life* each day. I pray you'll continue to live your dreams, change your world, and inspire others to do the same. You all have inspired me to grow as a person. Thank you for loving and supporting me.

To my parents who helped me to dream big and work hard, thanks for shaping my perspective and encouraging me to chase extraordinary dreams. Your unconditional love and support is never-ending.

To my brother Jeff, thank you for leading the way. Your creativity, hard work, determination, and success are awe-inspiring and have fueled my belief in living an *Extraordinary Life*. Your ability to dream bigger is changing our world.

To Pat and Cindy Sokoll, thank you for your never-ending support and friendship. Your family has made a great impact on my life, and I am eternally grateful for the love you have shown me and so many others through the years.

To my team I work with each day, thank you for all you do in helping me and so many others to live an *Extraordinary Life*. Your daily contributions of effort, sacrifice, and hard work are highly appreciated. I value your support greatly.

To the clients we serve, thank you for your support, belief, and investment in what we offer. Without you, these thoughts and ideas would be just more information without any transformation. But because of you, we see the transformation that comes from them when they are put to good use.

To all the other partners, friends, and family (who are too many to list) who helped me to become the man I am today, I say thank you. Without your support, my life wouldn't be extraordinary. Your encouragement, feedback, and assistance have helped me to realize my dreams and to establish new peaks to climb.

Writing this book has been a testament to everything I wrote in it. I truly believe I am living my calling, engaging in my dreams, agreeing to make hard choices, deciding to fail forward, expanding my perspective, and resolving to achieve the goals I set a long time ago.

This book is a fulfillment of my dreams, and to this I give all the glory to God, who inspired my thoughts and who gave me the courage and words to write it. Without my faith in God, I would have nothing, even if I had it all. I hope this book inspires you to strengthen your faith and that it brings you closer to your purpose in life.

ABOUT THE AUTHOR

David Bush
Extraordinary Results Coach

Through his coaching business and motivational speaking, David Bush inspires others to design and live extraordinary lives. His passion for developing exceptional leaders, teams, and organizations translates into a high-energy and powerful message that empowers individuals to live their dreams and change their world.

David's captivating message and life planning process on how ordinary people can live extraordinary lives has become a life operating system for many influential leaders.

After succeeding as a former all-American collegiate athlete on the University of South Dakota's football team and graduating with a degree in mass communication, David pursued a professional football career, landing a starting role with the Iowa Barnstormers of the Arena Football League in Des Moines, Iowa. After four years of playing professional football and two trips to the World Championship game ('96 and '97 Arena Bowl), David entered the world of mortgage banking and quickly became a top-producing mortgage consultant and business owner of a regional mortgage brokerage.

After ten years in mortgage banking, David ventured into the world of peak performance coaching and began coaching entrepreneurs to live their dreams and change their world. He now leads a team of certified coaches who coach thousands of individuals.

He is a highly sought-after business coach and motivational speaker who inspires audiences with stories of transformation and strategies that lead to extraordinary success and significance.

With a unique blend of humor, insightful storytelling, and take-home success strategies, David entertains and challenges audiences to become extraordinary in everything they do. Industry leaders and organizations from across the nation have called on David to coach them and their teams to extraordinary levels of success and significance.

David and his wife Kristen have three beautiful children, Cassidy, Morgan, and Beau.